THE PATRIOT WAR
ALONG THE
NEW YORK-CANADA
BORDER

THE
PATRIOT WAR
ALONG THE
NEW YORK-CANADA
BORDER

Raiders and Rebels

SHAUN J. MCLAUGHLIN

THE
History
PRESS

Published by The History Press
Charleston, SC 29403
www.historypress.net

Copyright © 2012 by Shaun J. McLaughlin
All rights reserved

First published 2012

Manufactured in the United States

ISBN 978.1.60949.465.0

Library of Congress Cataloging-in-Publication Data

McLaughlin, Shaun J.
The Patriot War along the New York/Canada border : raiders and rebels / Shaun J.
McLaughlin.
p. cm.
Includes bibliographical references and index.
ISBN 978-1-60949-465-0
1. Canada--History--Rebellion, 1837-1838. 2. New York (State)--History, Military--19th
century. I. Title.
F1032.M45 2012
971.03'8--dc23
2011047613

Contents

CONTENTS

Preface

The undeclared war between the United States and the Canadian colonies, mainly between December 1837 and December 1838—the so-called Patriot War—was a historical oddity. Not a war between nations, it was a war of ideals fought by like-minded people against the greatest military power of the time.

Rebellions in Lower Canada (now Quebec) and Upper Canada (now Ontario) flared up in November and December, respectively, in 1837. The British army and colonial militia quickly extinguished the uprisings. The ill-prepared rebels lacked the training and strength to prevail. The insurgency should have ended before Christmas. It did not.

The defeated rebels fled to the United States, where Americans of all social classes embraced them as heroes. Due to a unique confluence of American history and economics, tens of thousands of people offered money, provisions, arms and sometimes their lives in the pursuit of Canadian freedom. Many Americans regarded the English—still much despised—as despots to be driven from the continent once and for all.

The administration of President Martin Van Buren never endorsed or aided the conflict. American people, not the American government, declared war on Britain. The officers and men in the volunteer armies saw themselves as freedom fighters engaged in a just and noble cause. While land speculators infiltrated the senior ranks, the majority of men who fought, died and hanged acted on altruistic ideals, however misguided their mission may have been.

The Patriot War raged along the Great Lakes and St. Lawrence River from Michigan to Vermont. This book focuses on the contributions and sacrifices of key people in eastern Upper Canada and the border counties of New York State from Buffalo to Ogdensburg.

I collected the material in this book over years from sources too numerous to mention. A few stand out. I applaud the legion of New York historians and volunteers, such as those at the Thousand Islands Museum in Clayton, for compiling so much local history. I also owe a debt to the helpful people at the Mississippi Mills Public Library in Almonte, Ontario, for bringing in rare books I requested through interlibrary loan. Library and Archives Canada in Ottawa provided a wealth of material related to the Patriot War, including rare original copies of memoirs by American participants.

I am grateful to James Eagan and Roberta Calhoun-Eagan of Canandaigua, New York, for their help over the years compiling information on Bill Johnston's life. And a big thank-you to my wife, Amelia Ah You, for her skillful preparation of digital images for this book.

Lastly, I thank Whitney Tarella, commissioning editor at The History Press, for her guidance during this project.

1
Setting the Scene

The fact that bands of Canadian colonists in Upper and Lower Canada took up arms in the pursuit of responsible government is not surprising given the political realities of 1837. That a legion of Americans took up their cause with force and vigor is, on the surface, puzzling.

A two-tiered government ran the colonies of Upper Canada (now Ontario) and Lower Canada (now Quebec). Each had a legislative assembly elected by voters. Both had an all-powerful executive council made up of prominent citizens, headed by a lieutenant governor appointed by the Crown. The executive council could and did disregard advice and legislation from the elected assembly.

By 1837, both colonial executive councils represented an oligarchy of wealthy men, judges and high-ranking military officers. Rife with nepotism and patronage, they ran the colonies often for their members' profit. In Upper Canada, people called them the Family Compact. The Lower Canada equivalent was the Château Clique.

In Upper Canada, the Family Compact aligned with the Anglican Church, while the majority of residents belonged to other churches. In Lower Canada, the Anglican, English-speaking Château Clique had little in common with the Francophone and Catholic majority. Religious tension exacerbated the linguistic and political divide.

In both colonies, political parties arose to argue for democratic reform. More than once, these parties formed a majority in the legislative assemblies. The executive councils ignored them or, worse, passed laws that enflamed them. Eventually, a minority of reformers in both colonies counseled open rebellion as the only path to representative government. The mood in Canada matched the temper in America in 1775, when colonists fired the first shots of the Revolutionary War.

While Canadian politics fumed in 1837, the United States' society seethed with its own discontent. Between 1780 and 1837, the U.S. population rose from 2,780,400 to over 16,000,000. The count of states doubled from thirteen to twenty-six. Settlement had pushed civilization from the coastal plains west past the Mississippi River.

After fifty-six years of growth and prosperity, America hit a wall in 1837. Rampant land speculation combined with a sudden distrust of banks and the new monetary innovation—paper money—led to the Panic of 1837. English banks called in loans made to U.S. banks. Those banks held little real money—their assets being notes based on landholdings—and failed. Fortunes disappeared. Unemployment spiked. A five-year recession began.

Besides financial upheaval, the 1830s saw a steady series of new social experiments and clashes of ideals. Organizations formed to better American society morally and socially. New ideals—temperance, trade unions, education reform, penal reform, asylums, abolition and female suffrage—threatened established ideas.

Following the Texas Revolution (1835–1836), many Americans, especially young men, envisioned themselves as new crusaders, gallant fighters for democracy. (That the Texas Revolution had much to do with Mexico's prohibition of slavery was not well known then.)

In 1837, Americans along the border from Maine to Wisconsin still harbored enmity for the British government. Though fifty-six years had passed since fighting ceased in the American Revolution and twenty-three years since the War of 1812 ended, people in those states wanted the continent purged of any vestige of English despotism. And people blamed the English banks for causing the Panic of 1837.

Americans had no quarrel with Canadian colonists, who were kith and often kin. Immigration controls being rudimentary, citizens flowed between the nations at will. Cross-border business connections and marriages were commonplace.

When you add the Texas Revolution's romanticism to a nation awash in new ideas and combine that with the destabilizing effects of a recession and a deep-seated grudge against the British, it is easy to understand why Americans took up the Canadian rebels' cause. Brothers in difficult times, the Canadian rebellion offered an opportunity for young men to be heroes and old men to kick out the monarchists.

2

The Rebellion Begins

October–December 1837

Heated debate over democratic reforms morphed into armed rebellion first in Lower Canada. While Americans had little involvement in that conflict, the bloody reprisals by the British army, exaggerated by the American press, awakened the Spirit of '76 in the border states.

The principal agitator for political reform in Lower Canada was Louis-Joseph Papineau, fifty-one, an elected assembly member since 1808 (at just twenty-two). His continued insistence that government must be controlled by elected representatives, not appointees, alienated him from the English elite but made him the darling of discontented colonists. Papineau and his supporters, who called themselves *les Patriotes*, began to organize paramilitary cells in 1837.

Dr. Wolfred Nelson, forty-six, and Dr. Robert Nelson, forty-four, acted as his generals. As Anglophones advocating for the rights of the Francophone majority, the Nelson brothers were a rarity in Lower Canada.

The rebellion started as civil disobedience, not an act of war.

On October 23, 1837, five thousand Patriotes from six counties assembled near St. Charles, south of Montreal, in a peaceful protest against English political restrictions, despite a law forbidding such gatherings. Talk of reform, not war, filled the two-day event. The assembly adopted a set of American-style republican resolutions and dispersed peacefully.

In response, the colonial government overreacted and charged Papineau, Wolfred Nelson and two dozen regional leaders with treason on November 16, 1837, issuing arrest warrants.

L'Assemblée des six-comtés, by Charles Alexander Smith (1890), depicts the meeting in 1837 that caused Britain to arrest Patriote leaders, thus sparking the Patriot War.

Patriote leaders took refuge in the rebel-held village of Saint-Denis, southeast of Montreal, and prepared for a fight. The British obliged by sending Colonel Charles Gore, forty-four, and three hundred regulars to subdue them. Gore marched his force through mud, cold and freezing rain and confronted eight hundred dry and determined rebel fighters early on November 23, 1837.

The British force had the option to back off. No one had yet fired a shot. No one had died. Had the colonial establishment chosen diplomacy instead of brute force and compromise instead of intolerance, there may not have been a Patriot War. Demonstrating typical English colonial arrogance, Colonel Gore ordered his men forward and ignited a shooting war. After a day of fighting, with ammunition running low and his men weather-weary, Gore ordered a retreat.

The Patriotes won the first round, but victory proved ethereal. They lacked the means to sustain a defense of Saint-Denis. Papineau and many followers fled to Vermont.

Two days later, Colonel George Wetherall, forty-nine, with 420 regulars, attacked Saint-Charles. The Patriote defenders consisted of just 60 to 80 armed men. Wetherall's troops charged and quickly overran the defenses, setting buildings afire. Some rebels retreated, while a few raised their hands. As the infantry walked toward the surrendering Patriotes, rebel snipers opened fire, killing three soldiers. This treachery enraged the British, who then slaughtered every Patriote fighter they found—56 in all.

On November 30, 1837, Colonel Gore returned to Saint-Denis. The Patriotes had dispersed. The town surrendered without a fight. Out of spite, the English sacked the town and set fifty homes aflame.

On December 14, 1837, General John Colborne, First Baron Seaton, forty-nine, commander in chief of British armed forces in North America, led an army of 1,500 to the village of Saint-Eustache, west of Montreal. The redcoats faced 800 mostly unarmed Patriotes.

Most rebels dispersed. Jean-Olivier Chénier, thirty-one, a local physician, mustered a core of determined fighters and barricaded a convent, church, rectory and manor in the village center. Colborne, with his vastly superior force and artillery, systematically overran each building occupied by Chénier's men until only the church remained in rebel hands.

The infantry smashed in a door and set a fire to drive the Patriotes out. As rebels jumped from the burning church, soldiers picked them off, including Chénier. The battle left seventy Patriotes and three British men dead. For days following, militia units looted and burned homes in Saint-Eustache and neighboring villages, while the troops torched property of known rebel leaders.

UPPER CANADA IGNITES

The Upper Canada raiders and rebels who transformed the Canada–United States border into a war zone in 1838 can credit one diminutive Scotsman for starting the fight: William Lyon Mackenzie.

Driven by uncompromising political principles and a hatred of elitism, William Lyon spent his adult life trying to bring political reform to Upper Canada.

Mackenzie rose to prominence among reformers through his newspaper, the *Colonial Advocate*. Unlike newspapers of today, it served largely to get his opinions into circulation. (If alive today, he'd be a political blogger or talk show host.)

Drawing of William Lyon Mackenzie, circa 1850.

In January 1829, he won a seat in the colonial assembly. Because of his continued Family Compact criticism, the loyalist-dominated assembly voted three times to expel him, and each time he returned in the next election.

He became the first mayor of the new city of Toronto on March 27, 1834, but lost the 1835 election. In the pages of a second publication, the *Constitution*, Mackenzie continued to advocate for reform. But he grew increasingly impatient and uncompromising. He toured the rural country around Toronto organizing groups of potential rebels. His views on democracy found favor among farmers of American origin.

When Mackenzie learned the rebellion in Lower Canada had started, he commanded his troops to gather north of Toronto for a march on that city. With no armed forces in the local barracks, William Lyon felt his men could beat any militia assembled against them, especially in a surprise attack.

From counties surrounding Toronto, rebel captains and lieutenants marched bands of ill-equipped and poorly trained recruits toward the city. A second regiment of three hundred rebels under command of American-born Dr. Charles Duncombe, forty-five, gathered near Brantford, southwest of Toronto, and marched to join Mackenzie.

By December 4, between seven and eight hundred of Mackenzie's rebels, dubbed the Patriots, gathered on Toronto's outskirts by a tavern owned by John Montgomery. (While a reform sympathizer, Montgomery was no rebel—at least not then.) Though the rebels temporarily had the upper hand, they did not make a decisive early move.

Toronto Slow to React

Spies kept the lieutenant governor, Sir Francis Bond Head, forty-four, informed of Mackenzie's activities. Bond Head considered Mackenzie no more dangerous than a squawking parrot and did nothing to prepare for Upper Canada's defense. He even sent his one regiment of regulars to Lower Canada to help restore order there.

Not everyone shared the lieutenant governor's optimism. Colonel James FitzGibbon, fifty-seven, a veteran of the War of 1812 and Toronto militia commander, knew a rebel assault on Toronto was inevitable. Bond Head refused to let FitzGibbon prepare a defense, but he would not back down.

FitzGibbon contacted 126 men he could trust who had militia training and implored them to gather at the Parliament House should they hear

Right: Image of Sir Francis Bond Head.

Below: Drawing by Adrian Sharp depicting the shooting of Lieutenant Colonel Robert Moodie at Montgomery's Tavern, December 4, 1837.

Drawing depicting John Powell escaping from the rebels at Montgomery's Tavern, December 5, 1837.

the college bell ring. He told Bond Head of this plan and advised him that he would go ahead whether Bond Head consented or not. Bond Head weakly relented.

On December 4, Lieutenant Colonel Robert Moodie, fifty-nine, rode from Toronto to the tavern to investigate. He foolishly fired his pistol at a group of sentries, who shot him dead on the spot. Witnesses spread the alarming news.

A city alderman, John Powell, twenty-eight, rode north on December 5 to investigate. Mackenzie, armed with a pistol, took Powell and a second man prisoner. Powell surrendered peacefully and assured Mackenzie, when asked, that he carried no weapons. Being a novice rebel, Mackenzie accepted a gentleman's word and handed Powell over to his chief military officer, Anthony Anderson.

Like many 1837 rebels, Anderson, forty-one, had loyalist roots. Born in New Brunswick, he came to Upper Canada in 1809 with his parents. He joined the army as a teenager during the War of 1812 and fought at the Battle of Lundy's Lane in 1814. Given one hundred acres for his service, he began farming. He married Elizabeth Taylor in 1816 and sired eleven children. Mackenzie appointed him captain for his military experience.

Powell, acting passive and non-threatening, took a moment to size up the rebels' strength and then drew two loaded pistols from his coat. He shot Anderson in the back, killing him instantly. The second pistol, fired inches from William Lyon's chest, misfired. Powell galloped to Toronto and informed Colonel FitzGibbon of what had transpired, thus ending any Patriot hopes of a surprise. (Powell's heroics gained him the post of city mayor at the next election.)

The Shooting Starts

At dusk on December 5, Mackenzie rode a white pony at the head of his ragtag rebels. Near the city, a militia picket set up by Colonel FitzGibbon fired on the bigger rebel force. Rebel captain Samuel Lount lined his men up. The front ranks returned fire and dropped on their bellies instead of stepping aside or kneeling to reload, as was the custom. The ranks behind assumed those in front had fallen to musket balls and retreated in fear. Mackenzie and Lount hastened to the tavern and reassembled five hundred remaining men.

> One of the first militia officers inside the tavern was Jonas Jones. As a colonial judge, he later sentenced numerous Patriots to death.

The next day, William Lyon lost further advantage by robbing the mail courier in search of intelligence instead of pushing on to Toronto. That day, Colonel Allan MacNab, thirty-nine, arrived from Hamilton with sixty troops. Bond Head placed MacNab in charge of the defense of Toronto ahead of the much more experienced FitzGibbon (probably out of spite).

On December 7, MacNab's defensive force marched out to attack the rebels at the tavern. The two armies met in the early afternoon. The militia, supported by cannons, overpowered the rebels within an hour and sent them running like scared rabbits. MacNab arrested Montgomery and burned his tavern.

An estimated two hundred rebel officers and men fled to the United States. Many, including Lount, never made it to safety.

When he heard news of Mackenzie's defeat, Dr. Duncombe disbanded his force and also fled to America.

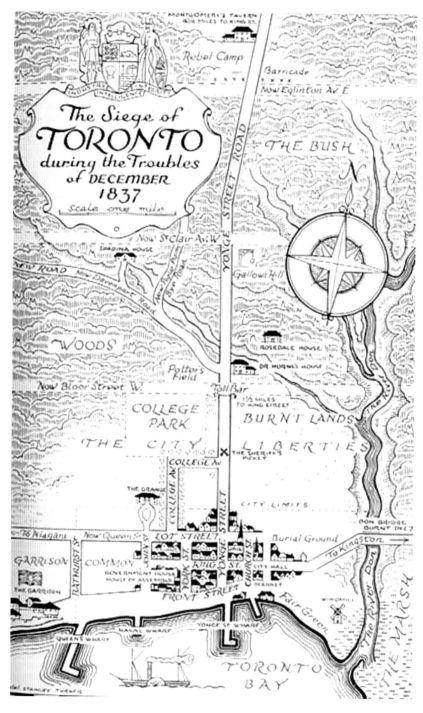

Illustrated map of Toronto by Stanley Turner depicting key locations during the December 1837 rebellion.

Bond Head issued a reward of £1,000 for Mackenzie's capture. The notice, printed in the *Upper Canada Herald* on December 19, 1837, described him as "a short man, wears a sandy colored wig, has small twinkling eyes that can look no man in the face—he is about 5 feet 4 or 5 inches in height." The notice also offered £500 for Samuel Lount, Silas Fletcher and David Gibson.

Running for his life, William Lyon traveled from one safe house to the next around the western end of Lake Ontario. Nearing the border, he met Samuel Chandler, a wagon maker. Born in Connecticut, Chandler was forty-eight with a wife and children. Though not a rebel, Chandler sympathized

Samuel Chandler, circa 1850. *University of Western Ontario Archives.*

with Mackenzie and guided him to the Niagara River shore and across to Grand Island, New York. Chandler's fateful choice shifted the course of his life.

William Lyon left behind a colony in upheaval. The rebellion gave the conservative elite an excuse to crush its political opponents. Colonial leaders branded all reform advocates as rebels. Loyalist mobs terrorized the colony, tacitly encouraged by the Family Compact. Good and loyal citizens fled to America, many into the ranks of the rebels.

Mackenzie arrived in Buffalo on December 10 knowing his rebellion had failed but not yet aware that the Patriot War had just begun.

3

Americans Join the Fight

December 1837

Newspaper accounts (often greatly exaggerated) of British army massacres in Lower Canada enraged freedom-loving Americans even before Patriot refugees landed on New York State's safe shores. A knot of prominent men in Buffalo had followed the rise of revolution in the Canadian colonies and knew well the name William Lyon Mackenzie.

Mackenzie met a populace primed for action. Among the civic leaders who championed the rebellion, Dr. Cyrenius Chapin, sixty-eight, took an early leadership role. He loathed the English, having grown up during the American Revolution. During the War of 1812, he headed a band of freebooters who pillaged Upper Canada's Niagara region so regularly that Americans dubbed his gang "Doctor Chapin and the Forty Thieves." During a raid on Buffalo in 1814, the British captured Chapin and held him until the war ended.

In Buffalo, Chapin swept up the fugitive Scot and made him his houseguest. Chapin organized a public meeting the next evening, December 11, in a Buffalo theater. Supporters packed the place. According to an account in the *Buffalo Commercial Advertiser*, noted by Charles Lindsey in his 1862 biography of William Lyon, Chapin worked the audience preacher-style.

"Our neighbors in the North," said Dr. Chapin, "are at war, fighting for liberty. I have men now under my protection, at my house, on whose life a price is set, and whom I am bound to protect."

"Who are they?" was the prompt inquiry from the audience.

"One of them is William L. Mackenzie," he replied.

At this announcement, the newspaper reported, "the vast assembly burst into a thunder of applause. We never saw such a scene," the reporter added, "never heard such a shout of exultation." When the outburst subsided, Dr. Chapin continued his hortatory talk.

"Fellow citizens, Mackenzie's life is in our power—he has thrown himself upon our protection—will you protect him?"

"We will," was the unanimous response.

> *To-morrow night, he shall address you. I am an old man; but at the hazard of my life I will protect those who throw themselves upon my hospitality. If any scoundrels, for the sake of the $4,000 reward that is offered for him, shall undertake to get him, they must first walk over my body. I want six strong, brave young men, as good sons as God has got among us, to go to my house tonight, for fear of any attempt on the part of the loyalists.*

Chapin waved a Bowie knife, a potent reminder of the Alamo martyrs. One hundred volunteers rose, and Chapin picked the first six to mount the stage.

As Chapin promised, Mackenzie spoke at the same theater the next night. A fiery and accomplished orator, the bantam-sized rebel leader knew his audience well. The majority had either fought during the American Revolution or the War of 1812 or claimed kinship with veterans of those wars.

To a packed house estimated at three thousand people (the population of Buffalo was then twenty-five thousand), Mackenzie explained the rebellion's causes. He compared the suffering of Canadians to the "same evils" that had caused the thirteen colonies to break allegiance from England.

With the audience primed, Thomas Jefferson Sutherland, thirty-six, addressed the throng next. He'd watched the Canadian revolution develop and supported it with enthusiasm. A week earlier (December 5), he had traveled to Toronto with a letter of support, which Mackenzie read to his troops the next day at Montgomery's tavern.

Sutherland fancied himself a natural commander of men and fully expected to be a general in any force raised to support Canadian freedom. That night, he stated he intended to form an army of liberation. He requested men, money, ammunition and weapons. The response was immediate and generous.

The focus shifted the next day to the Eagle Tavern, one of the finest stagecoach stops outside New York City. Owned by Elisha A. Huntley, the establishment on Main Street in Buffalo became, for a time, the Patriot headquarters. Their flag (a tricolor with two stars) flew from the tavern's flagpole.

Drawing of the Eagle Tavern in Buffalo, circa 1825. For a time in 1837–38, it served as the Patriot headquarters.

That evening, December 13, Mackenzie and Sutherland met in the tavern to plan a war. With them were Dr. John Rolph, forty-four, and Rensselaer Van Rensselaer, thirty-five.

Dr. John Rolph

English-born John Rolph was called to the Upper Canada bar in 1821 and became a doctor in 1829. Drawn to politics, he held a legislative assembly seat from 1824 to 1830 as a reformer. In 1834, he became an alderman for the new city of Toronto. In 1836, he won a seat in the assembly again.

Rolph did not aid William Lyon Mackenzie in his initial war plans; however, Mackenzie kept him informed. Rolph helped set the actual Toronto attack date. During the fateful days of December 4 to 7, 1837, he worked as a double agent. Enlisted as a peace envoy by Sir Francis Bond Head, he visited the rebels and passed battle instructions to Samuel Lount. On December 11, Bond Head posted a £500 reward for Rolph. The prudent doctor had already fled to Buffalo.

Rensselaer Van Rensselaer

Rensselaer Van Rensselaer came from one of the most influential families in upstate New York. Men with his surname ranked among the elite in politics and the military. His grand-uncle, Stephen Van Rensselaer III, owned a massive estate in the Hudson River Valley, graduated from Harvard, founded the Rensselaer Polytechnic Institute in 1824 (it still exists), served as the state lieutenant governor and commanded an army during the War of 1812.

Van Rensselaer's father, Solomon, served as a decorated colonel under Stephen in the War of 1812 and later as a U.S. congressman and the postmaster of Albany.

As a young man, Van Rensselaer showed promise. In October 1829, he joined the diplomatic staff of General William Henry Harrison, minister to the republic of Colombia. (Harrison became the ninth and shortest-serving president in 1841.) Once back home, Van Rensselaer became proprietor of the *Albany Evening Advertiser*.

On December 11, 1838, while in Buffalo on business, Van Rensselaer met Sutherland. The latter immediately tried to recruit him into the Patriot cause. Sutherland offered to resign his position as Patriot army commander in chief to make way for Van Rensselaer. Sutherland believed the cause needed a person better known than he to impart "a proper tone to the enterprise." Van Rensselaer accepted at the request of Mackenzie.

Van Rensselaer, who had no military experience, later admitted he accepted the offer because he wanted to free Canada like Sam Houston liberated Texas. In retrospect, his tenure as Patriot general was a desperate grasp for glory to earn his status in the Van Rensselaer clan of high achievers.

If Sutherland and Mackenzie didn't then know of Van Rensselaer's reputation as a lush, they soon learned the hard way.

Navy Island Occupied

The Patriot leaders agreed to occupy Navy Island and make it the seat of a provisional government in exile. The 316-acre island in the Niagara River, not far from the mighty falls, belonged to Upper Canada.

The legality of preparing for a war on Canada was debatable. The U.S. Neutrality Act forbade anyone from attacking another country at peace with America. Planning for war and gathering weapons fell into a gray area. Certainly, no one tried to stop the waves of Patriots marching through Buffalo

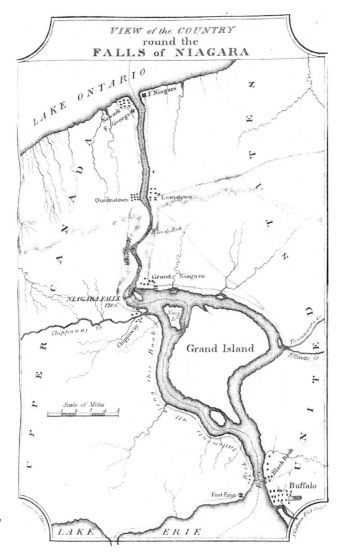

Map of the Niagara River including Navy Island, by John Melish, circa 1812. *David Rumsey Map Collection.*

to the Schlosser Harbor on the Niagara River. Once on Navy Island, the Patriots stood beyond the reach of American law—until they returned.

On December 14, Mackenzie and newly appointed General Van Rensselaer landed on Navy Island by way of Grand Island with twenty-four volunteers and two small cannons. As the news of the occupation spread, small groups of Canadian refugees and American volunteers from across the state journeyed to Navy Island. Surgeons came to tend to the wounded and the sick. Engineers helped design fortifications. Former military officers advised on defense. Recruits brought cannons stolen from New York State arsenals (twenty-four in all), rifles, muskets and ammunition. Brigadier General Sutherland arrived with a company.

The island's north side boasted high banks with a good view of mainland Canada. The Patriots immediately dug in their artillery there and commenced bombarding the Canadian shore.

Van Rensselaer strutted about the island, a cutlass in one hand and brandy in the other. As weeks passed, he refused to divulge his plans (probably because he had none). His drunkenness was obvious and his cowardice suspected. Men sought action but found only boredom and crude huts for shelter from the cold and snow. Even as new recruits joined the island's defenders, a steady stream of deserters departed for home.

At its peak, the island's Patriot force numbered approximately six hundred, almost equally Canadian and American. Their ranks included men who went on to play larger roles in the Patriot War: Samuel Chandler, Benjamin Lett, Benjamin Wait, Bill Johnston and Lester Hoadley. (Hoadley later served in the western Patriot army.)

Upper Canada Fights Back

In Toronto, news of the Navy Island occupation took Lieutenant Governor Bond Head by surprise. He thought the revolt ended on December 7. He sent Colonel Allan MacNab to defend the Niagara frontier. Militia, volunteers and native warriors joined MacNab and swelled his force to over two thousand. The colonel set up his own artillery and fired on the island, with little effect. (Accounts say weeks of bombardment killed one Patriot and wounded several others.)

The opposing forces reached a stalemate. The swift river current on the side of Navy Island facing the colony prevented an easy attack from Canada by

Engraving of an 1842 print by William Henry Bartlett showing Navy Island from the Canadian side.

Painting by J.B. Read, 1838, of the attack on the *Caroline* viewed from the U.S. shore near Schlosser, New York.

water. With MacNab's superior force in place, the Patriots had no chance of advancing further at that point.

If MacNab had patiently held his ground, as his orders from Bond Head stated, the Patriot War may have fizzled out that winter. But MacNab, arrogant by nature and angered by the Patriot cannon fire, sanctioned a military action that did more to boost Mackenzie's support than any of his fiery speeches.

On December 29, 1837, Captain Andrew Drew, forty-five, acting on MacNab's orders, rowed across the icy river in darkness with sixty armed militiamen in small boats and boarded the Patriots' rented supply ship, the *Caroline*, at Schlosser. A handful of men slept on the steamer. Only the sentry carried a musket.

Drew's raiders stormed the ship and killed a black American sailor named Amos Durfee in the mêlée. He became the war's first American casualty—but not the last.

Drew's men towed the *Caroline* into the current and set it afire. The blazing craft grounded on rocks and broke apart, its pieces plummeting over the falls.

Americans saw the British attack on an American ship in a U.S. port as an assault on their sovereignty. While President Martin Van Buren accepted a lame apology from the colony and shrugged off the incursion, U.S. citizens sent money and ammunition to Mackenzie. American volunteers soon outnumbered Canadians in the Patriot army.

MacNab and Drew ignited a patriotic fire in Americans that took more than a year to die down. Burning the *Caroline* was a rash military act. It mutated a bungled revolt near Toronto into a yearlong undeclared border war that cost the English treasury millions of dollars to wage.

> The *Caroline* attack stands as an early example of a preemptive strike by one peaceful nation on another.

For his part in the unsanctioned raid, Queen Victoria knighted Colonel MacNab in March 1838.

4

New Leaders Recruited

January 1838

The opposing forces at Navy Island continued to bombard each other for two weeks following the *Caroline* affair. Boredom compounded by cold made Van Rensselaer's dithering unbearable to the rebels. Patriot fighters steadily deserted. On January 13, 1838, Van Rensselaer abandoned Navy Island and withdrew his men to Buffalo.

General Sutherland departed on January 7, 1838, for the Patriots' western front in Ohio and Michigan. (Battles fought in that arena are not part of this book.)

The retreat from Navy Island did not bring the war to an end. Old and new leaders gathered with new plans.

SILAS FLETCHER

Born in Chesterfield, New Hampshire, Fletcher became a farmer north of Toronto. He married Isabelle Sutherland in 1809. They had fifteen children together. His reward notice described him as six feet tall and straight, with a sallow complexion, black whiskers and hair turning gray. He tended to speak in "a peculiar and quick manner" and be "very quick in his motions." As a rebel captain, Silas Fletcher distinguished himself as a competent officer and top recruiter, despite being illiterate.

In the latter days of December 1837 and into January 1838, Fletcher, fifty-seven, traveled the northern counties of New York, proving himself equally capable at recruiting Americans. Many men at Navy Island can credit Fletcher for pointing the way. After the *Caroline* affair, his job became easier.

BILL JOHNSTON

Sketch of William Johnston by Benson Lossing in his book *Pictorial Field-Book of the War of 1812*, 1869.

William "Bill" Johnston, fifty-five—whose scallywag and scofflaw ways in later years came to the attention of Queen Victoria and at least five U.S. presidents—spent thirty years as a loyal subject. Then, all hell broke loose.

In 1781, Bill's parents, James (originally from Belfast) and Catherine Pegg (of Dutch descent from New Jersey) joined United Empire Loyalists in flight from the newly independent United States to colonial Canada. Separated from James, Catherine stayed for two years in Trois Riviere, Lower Canada (Quebec), where Bill was born. In the spring of 1784, she and her young family arrived in Ernesttown (now named Bath), twelve miles west of Kingston.

In 1785, her English sergeant husband joined them and began the task of building a farm in a primal forest. With grandfather William and eventually twelve children to help, the family prospered.

At sixteen, Bill was apprenticed to a blacksmith. It was a formative period for the young farm lad. Men gathered at the village smithy to discuss issues of the day. He stayed for six years, building his muscles and extending his knowledge of business and political intrigues.

At twenty-two, he became a potash manufacturer, capitalizing on a plentiful supply of ashes from burned forests. He shipped it by bateaux to Montreal, thus beginning his long association with the St. Lawrence River.

At five feet, ten inches, he was broad at the shoulders, barrel-chested, thick-necked and strong from a life of hard work. He had a baritone voice and penetrating blue-gray eyes. He used his size and demeanor to get his way.

By twenty-four, he was plying eastern Lake Ontario as captain of his own schooner. While he often carried legitimate cargo, he just as often shipped contraband, thus beginning his decades as a successful smuggler. By early Upper Canada government estimates, 75 to 90 percent of tea consumed in the colony came from smugglers.

On one trip to America, he met an attractive milliner named Sarah Ann Randolph. They were married in 1807 or early 1808.

After five years of smuggling, Bill amassed enough profit to buy a Kingston store valued at an estimated $12,000—a small fortune in that era. In 1811, he moved Ann (no one called her Sarah) and his young family to Kingston, then the military and economic hub of Upper Canada. His store was a meeting place for critics of local politics and a rendezvous for American travelers.

By his thirtieth birthday, he was a prosperous merchant and on his way to becoming a pillar of Upper Canada society. But suspicion, intolerance and fear at the start the War of 1812, coupled with Bill's independent nature, changed his life and the history of the Thousand Islands.

The United States declared war on Britain in June 1812 and attacked its colonies in Canada. With Canada's military significantly outnumbered, the war threw Kingston into a patriotic and jingoistic frenzy. Colonial authorities viewed criticism with deep suspicion.

Johnston rarely kept his opinions to himself. For one, he spoke out against the injustice of holding American civilians in the filthy Kingston jails. The colonial army refused to let American citizens return home during the war.

The colony expected all men from ages eighteen to forty-five to join the militia. Johnston enlisted but didn't stay long. One story relates that a captain reprimanded him one day, probably for criticizing the authorities, and struck Bill with a cane. Not one to suffer fools or abuse, Bill gave the officer a thrashing. That led to a court-martial and a brief jail term.

Johnston relieved himself of his militia obligation by convincing a brother (we don't know his name) to step in for him. Historian Dr. William Canniff, in his 1869 tome *History of the Settlement of Upper Canada*, wrote:

> *There was not at this time any doubt of his loyalty. It was natural he should desire to attend to his business in Kingston, which at this time was*

lucrative. And there does not appear that he employed his brother in other than good faith.

Johnston traveled on business to the United States—a suspicious undertaking on its own. He returned to learn that his brother had deserted, thus requiring him to rejoin. Canniff continues, "Even now it does not appear that the authorities of Kingston suspected his loyalty for they desired that he should take his place in the ranks, which his brother had forsaken."

Bill refused to rejoin his militia unit. He was arrested and soon released.

In May 1813, Colonel Richard Cartwright, fifty-five, regimental commander in Kingston, decided to imprison Johnston for the war's duration, allegedly for spying. By order of Captain Mathew Clark, one of Bill's neighbors in Bath, Sergeant David Lockwood, one of Bill's boyhood friends, arrived at his store with a squad of soldiers. Canniff, who interviewed Lockwood three decades later, tells what happened next:

Upon the approach of the soldiers, Johnson [sic] shouted to Sergeant Lockwood, "I know what you are after but you won't get me yet," and immediately shut the door and turned the key. Lockwood raised his musket and with the butt knocked the door open in time to see Bill escaping by the back door. A close chase ensued into a back enclosure and Lockwood succeeded in catching him by the leg as he was passing through a window. Johnson then submitted and was conveyed a prisoner to the guard house within the jail. After being confined for some time, he escaped by breaking the jail, probably aided by sympathizers, for a good many thought he was badly treated.

Johnston always said no jail could hold him if he chose to leave, as he proved often.

In a birch bark canoe with five American refugees, he crossed the lake to Sackets Harbor, New York, the American navy headquarters on Lake Ontario. Upon his arrival, he pledged himself to Commodore Isaac Chauncey, fifty-nine, the fleet commander.

A subsequent letter from Johnston said:

Up until that time, I solemnly declare, I had no communication with the American army or navy, or any individual to my knowledge, by whom any information was likely to be conveyed to the enemy, to the injury of His Majesty's subjects or those of his realm.

The government confiscated Bill's store, house and four hundred acres of farmland near Bath. In turn, Bill promised to be a lifelong thorn in Great Britain's side for his mistreatment—and he kept his word.

One naval officer, and a fellow defender at Sackets Harbor, was sailing master William Vaughan. While compatriots then, he and Bill became enemies later.

That old adage "from the frying pan into the fire" sums up Bill's flight to the United States. The war seemed to follow him. Days after he smuggled his family to Sackets Harbor, Bill helped defend the town.

The American fleet had sailed away to attack Canada near Niagara. British general Sir George Prevost chose that time to sail into the harbor, guns blazing. On the twenty-ninth, Prevost's troops landed at Sackets Harbor. Fierce fighting ensued, with cannon fire and musket volleys from both sides. The invaders advanced well into town but couldn't dislodge the Americans. Prevost despaired of victory and departed.

Bill became a river marauder for Commodore Chauncey. He gathered crews of American river men. They sculled throughout the Thousand Islands and the eastern end of Lake Ontario, spying and attacking bateaux carrying supplies to Upper Canada.

Johnston's men traveled in gigs, narrow and lightweight boats. Powered by six oarsmen, they darted between islands. When chased by enemy sailing craft (they had no steamers then), Bill's crew maneuvered their boats down tight channels or portaged them across an island to the far side.

In November 1813, seven thousand Americans commanded by General James Wilkinson headed down the St. Lawrence River in hundreds of Durham boats, part of a bold plan to invade Montreal. Wilkinson rode in Bill's gig.

British regulars and Canadian militia dogged the Americans, sniping from the shore and from boats at their rear. The Americans stopped their convoy to engage the pesky Canadians at a farm owned by John Crysler. Though outnumbered, they defeated the much larger American force. This encounter, known as the Battle of Crysler's Farm, forced the Americans to abandon the assault on Montreal.

By September 1814, the war on Lake Ontario had stalemated. Both sides built bigger warships hoping for naval superiority. The British prepared to launch the *St. Lawrence*, the mightiest craft on the Great Lakes with 112 guns (larger than Lord Nelson's famous flagship HMS *Victory*).

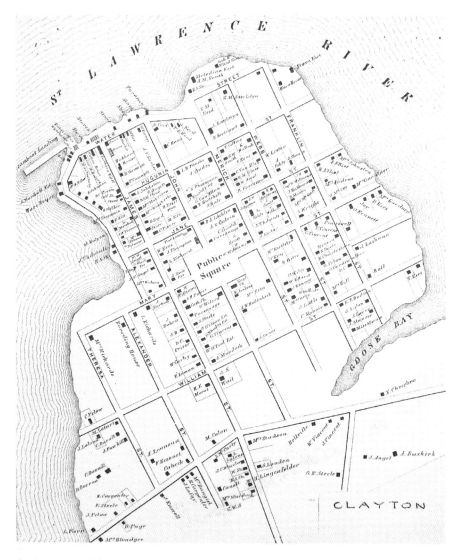

An 1864 map of Clayton, New York. One of three houses, top left, owned by S. (Samuel) Johnston once belonged to his father, Bill.

Bill joined a crew of five and crossed to Kingston one night in two boats. They snuck into Navy Bay in the shadow of old Fort Henry, intending to sink the big warship using a primitive naval mine. To their disappointment, the *St. Lawrence* had sailed earlier that day. The war ended that winter.

Following the war, Bill and his growing family settled for brief periods in Watertown, Cape Vincent and other northern New York towns. He struggled to regain the prosperity he had enjoyed before his exile from Canada. He moved to Clayton in 1834, his home for the rest of his long life.

There he established a shop on the waterfront and lived nearby in a cottage-like house facing the river. He continued smuggling goods to Canada while also working for the American revenue service. In an ironic twist, his job was to spy on Canadian smugglers coming into the United States.

Prosperity finally returned by 1837. If it hadn't been for the *Caroline's* destruction and Fletcher's visit to Jefferson County, Johnston might have remained a peaceful merchant and smuggler. But his fires of hatred for the monarchy still smoldered, and the Patriot cause became his own.

Bill Johnston visited Navy Island in early January 1838, bringing with him a nine-pound field cannon. There, Johnston first met Mackenzie (whom he admired) and Van Rensselaer (whom he quickly distrusted). Johnston rested three days and returned to Clayton briefly.

DONALD MCLEOD

Donald McLeod came to the Patriot cause at age fifty-nine with more war experience than any other Patriot officer. Born in Scotland, he joined the British navy in 1803 and switched to the infantry in 1808. He fought against Napoleon, including at Waterloo. As a sergeant in the War of 1812, he served at Queenston Heights, Crysler's Farm and Lundy's Lane—three pivotal victories for colonial Canada.

McLeod retired from the army and settled in Prescott, where he continued his life as a loyal citizen. He became a militia major, a schoolteacher and a newspaper publisher who championed political reform. Days following the rebel rout at Toronto in December 1837, a "Tory mob," as McLeod put it, trashed his printing office as a warning. He fled to the United States with Silas Fletcher. Angry at his treatment, McLeod traveled to Buffalo and joined Mackenzie's border war.

In a letter to his wife, McLeod spoke of his first Patriot mission:

> *I am at the head of 500 as brave men as ever handled a gun. I shall shortly be in Canada with them to pay the Tories a visit. Kiss each of the children for me. Give my respects to all true reformers. I have now travelled upwards of 500 miles, on the American side. The Citizens are the most generous and noble hearted people the world can produce.*

If we fail in setting Canada free, it will not be their fault; money, men and other means they have given with cheerful hearts. In fact their kindness will compel us to fight and conquer, whether or not. Farewell my Dear wife for the present. You shall hear from me every week. Your last injunction to me was never to fill a Coward's Grave. Depend upon it, my loving, brave and heroic wife.

DANIEL HEUSTIS

Daniel Heustis, from the cover of his 1848 memoirs.

Daniel Dunbar Heustis, thirty-one, was born on a farm in Coventry, Vermont, one of nine children. In 1816, the family moved to Westmoreland, New Hampshire, where his father died in 1825.

Heustis was five feet, ten inches tall with straight hair. He was passably handsome and tended to present an earnest expression.

In 1834, he settled in Watertown, New York, to work for his uncle James Wood manufacturing morocco (a fine-grained leather). In 1837, he went into business with a cousin trading West India goods and groceries.

His travels often took him to Upper Canada. Of Canadians, he later wrote:

They were harassed in a thousand ways, robbed of their dearest rights, plundered of their substance, and all their remonstrance's no more heeded than the idle wind. They were taxed, most exorbitantly, to support a host of proud, overbearing, insolent, and virtually irresponsible government-officers, in whose appointment they had no voice, and over whose conduct they could exercise no control or supervision.

The massacres of Patriotes in Lower Canada horrified Heustis. The *Caroline* incident inflamed him. The mild-mannered shopkeeper became militant. On January 10, 1838, he bid adieu to his wife and business partner to join the Patriots on Navy Island. He arrived one day too late but located Mackenzie and visited with him and his wife. Though Heustis had no military experience, William Lyon appointed him captain on the strength of his moral leadership.

DAVID GIBSON

Scottish-born David Gibson arrived in Canada in 1825 and found work as a surveyor. In 1828, he married his cousin Eliza Milne and began farming. In the 1830s, he became an avid reformer and won election to the assembly in 1834 and 1836. At thirty-three, he reluctantly joined Mackenzie's rebellion as a captain. He fled the debacle at Montgomery's tavern to New York. While he helped plan early Patriot campaigns, he was a nonviolent moderate at heart.

COUNCIL OF WAR HELD

On or about January 15, 1838, William Lyon Mackenzie, Rensselaer Van Rensselaer and David Gibson met in the Eagle Tavern's well-appointed private rooms over drinks with a clutch of new Patriot leaders: Bill Johnston, Donald McLeod and Daniel Heustis.

Mackenzie led the meeting, fresh from a brief jail term. American authorities arrested him in Buffalo days earlier for offenses under the Neutrality Act. Supporters quickly raised $5,000 for his bail.

Over dinner and drinks (Van Rensselaer was a lush and Johnston a teetotaler), the three new Patriot officers hatched a plan to take over Canada. Of all the

In a quirk of history, McLeod had helped defeat Van Rensselaer's great-uncle Stephen at the Battle of Queenston Heights in October 1812 and fought against Johnston at the Battle of Crysler's Farm in 1813. That day, all were allies.

attempts at Canadian liberation in 1838, their invasion plan had the greatest chance of success.

The strategy consisted of three parts. McLeod agreed to lead an army through the winter snows to attack Upper Canada from the west near Detroit. Johnston and Heustis intended to raise an army in upstate New York and invade Canada near Gananoque in the Thousand Islands. The Patriot leaders expected those assaults to draw the defenders from Fort Henry in Kingston, leaving the fort lightly guarded. Militant farmers would then capture the fort and control Kingston.

As the military center of Upper Canada, the fall of Fort Henry would cut the colony in two. A rebel success of that magnitude could have attracted thousands of armed American volunteers and discontented Canadians to the Patriot cause and changed the course of Canadian history.

The plan's architect remains in doubt. Van Rensselaer always claimed it was his strategy, but he had displayed no military sense to the point, and none after. Heustis and McLeod never stated in their memoirs who devised the plan. But it has Bill Johnston's signature all over it. Success required the participation of hundreds of dissident Canadians. Only Johnston knew the depth of discontent in rural counties around Kingston, and only Johnston had the contacts and credibility to organize a guerrilla force in that region.

They set February 22, George Washington's birthday, as the day to launch the coordinated raids.

Bill Johnston returned to Clayton. Gibson, Mackenzie and Mackenzie's wife, Isabel, accompanied Heustis to Watertown. McLeod began his march to Detroit.

Word of the coordinated plan reached Robert Nelson, then the Patriotes' principal military leader (Wolfred Nelson was in prison). He, too, prepared a raid across the border for February.

The icy grip of winter did little to quell the flames of war.

5

Hickory Island Occupied

February 1838

Patriot leaders circulated printed flyers across New York's northern counties calling on all lovers of liberty to contribute to the cause. Enthusiastic supporters offered sleighs, provisions, clothing and money. Patriot teams traveled the counties collecting promised articles and returned to the main depot at Watertown.

In towns and cities throughout Jefferson, Oswego and Onondaga Counties, companies of citizen soldiers gelled around community leaders and began to train for war.

For weapons, the Patriot leaders simply stole rifles and cannons from militia arsenals in Watertown, Batavia and Elizabethtown, often with guards turning a blind eye. Placed in sleighs, rebels shipped the rifles, powder and shot to Clayton or across the river to the countryside surrounding Kingston.

Heustis wrote:

> *We borrowed, without leave, about 700 stand of arms from the arsenal at Watertown. It was the general opinion, the next day, that the arms had gone towards Canada; but the U.S. Deputy Marshal, Jason Fairbanks, Esq., in his pursuit of them, went in an opposite direction, and before he had traveled many miles ruined a valuable horse, worth nearly as much as the guns. For future security, a guard was set over the arsenal. Nevertheless, some of the arms escaped on subsequent occasions, and it was mischievously reported that the sentinels were very useful in passing them out of the building. Eventually they were nearly all returned.*

The *Watertown Jeffersonian* downplayed the theft in its report:

> *The state arsenal in this village was broken open on the night of the 18th inst., and a quantity of arms taken therefrom; it is supposed their destination is Canada, as a large number of loyal Canadians were said to have arrived in the village the evening previous. We understand that the keeper, Mr. J. Fairbanks, Esq., has repaired to Albany to notify the proper authorities, and to receive such instructions as the exigencies of the case require. A reward of $250 is offered for the recovery of the property and the conviction of the offenders. It is not a little remarkable that the arms taken are of those taken from the British in the last war.*

According to Heustis, a grand jury investigated the theft of weapons but obtained little information. In his memoirs, Heustis related the testimony of a teamster named Carter from Clayton, a man occasionally employed by Bill Johnston:

> *Questioner: Are you acquainted with William Johnston?*
> *Carter: I am.*
> *Questioner: Have you been in his service recently?*
> *Carter: I have.*
> *Questioner: Was you at Watertown on that day of February?*
> *Carter: I was.*
> *Questioner: Did you carry a load from Watertown to French Creek?*
> *Carter: I did.*
> *Questioner: Where did you get that load?*
> *Carter: When I drove up to Gibson's hotel in the evening, a man came out and said he would take care of my horses. He was a large man, or else he was considerably bundled up. I gave up the horses to him and went in to warm me. In about half an hour the horses were again brought to the door. I went out, and the man told me to drive to French Creek as quick as possible.*
> *Questioner: What did your load consist of?*
> *Carter: I don't know.*
> *Questioner: Why didn't you look to see?*
> *Carter: I didn't want to know.*
> *Questioner: Was it light or heavy?*
> *Carter: It drawed pretty heavy.*
> *Questioner: What did you do with the load?*

Sketch of Clayton, New York, by Captain James Van Cleve, circa 1852, included in a travelers' handbook from the St. Lawrence Steamboat Company.

Carter: When I got to French Creek the next morning, I drove to Buzzell's hotel, where I stopped and went in to warm me. Being very cold, I remained some time. When I went out my team was standing at the door, but the sleigh had been unloaded. I then took my team and drove home, and that is all I know about it.

In the Midland District—the counties surrounding Kingston— hundreds of disgruntled farmers, men angry at the Family Compact's unequal and authoritarian rule, accepted arms and agreed to use them when summoned. Scores of Midland farmers had roots in the United States and had come to Canada lured by cheaper farmland. They retained their democratic ideals.

Though there is no historical paper trail to prove it, Bill Johnston likely handled the smuggling of arms to the Midland. For twenty-five years, he successfully smuggled tea to Upper Canada. Farmers bought the contraband and shipped it to market in hay wagons. It was a small matter to substitute weapons and ammunition. Once in Canada, the munitions vanished. Lieutenant Colonel Richard Bonnycastle, Fort Henry's militia commandant and Johnston's arch-enemy in 1838, later wrote in his posthumously published book, *Canada As It Was, Is and Will Be*: "The introduction of arms and ammunition into Canada for the use of the rebels was so well devised and executed, that but little of either was ever discovered."

Under the plan, Johnston's army of farmers would travel to Kingston in small groups on the pretext of going to market and lodge in inns and public houses. When the Patriots stormed Gananoque, Upper Canada, and

Watercolor of early Gananoque, Upper Canada, by Henry Francis Ainslie, 1839.

Fort Henry emptied in response, they were to set fire to specific buildings in Kingston as a further diversion and then take the fort.

Bill Johnston stationed hand-picked men among the fort's employees. It was their job to open the gates. One agent agreed to spike the cannons and blow up the fort's magazines, which contained primitive but deadly Congreve rockets.

While Johnston toiled in Clayton, General Rensselaer Van Rensselaer lounged in Watertown, pretending the battle strategy was his and annoying people who met him. A series of disputes with Mackenzie had estranged the two men to the point that the latter refused to have any further dealings with Van Rensselaer. Mackenzie wrote, "I cannot sail in a boat to be piloted as he thinks fit."

On February 17, 1838, General Van Rensselaer arrived in Clayton and took command, making Johnston his second. This did not sit well with the men gathering in Clayton, but no one mutinied.

As hundreds of raiders filled the small town, word of a pending onslaught crossed the river to Lieutenant Colonel Richard Bonnycastle.

ELIZABETH BARNETT

The most famous informant was Elizabeth Barnett, twenty-two. The American-born teacher lived in Gananoque. She paid a brief visit to American relatives in Lafargeville, south of Clayton, that February. People spoke of little else but a planned invasion. Worse, she learned the target was her beloved town.

Barnett cut her visit short on the pretext of illness and headed home in a horse-drawn cutter on February 21. She stopped briefly in Clayton to see the war preparations

Elizabeth Barnett in her later years.

firsthand and then crossed the frozen and windswept St. Lawrence River. Arriving near nightfall, she alerted Gananoque leaders. When she mentioned Bill Johnston's involvement, the townsfolk had fits. Women and children fled to the country for safety. Men gathered weapons. Couriers rode at a gallop to Kingston, Brockville and other towns to spread the warning.

Canadian historians paint Barnett as the Laura Secord of her era. (Secord warned James FitzGibbon, then a captain, about an American surprise attack during the War of 1812.) The truth is less dramatic.

Lieutenant Colonel Richard Bonnycastle had a network of spies in Canada and the United States. The public recruitment of an army and a total lack of secrecy were principal weakness of the Patriot war effort in New York State. Even the most myopic English spy had plenty to report. Bonnycastle wrote that he knew of the Patriot plans three days ahead—well before Barnett's message reached him—and to a level of detail far beyond what she could have told him. (He does not mention Barnett in his memoirs.)

Also, by that point, an invasion of Canada was as predictable as a sunrise. On the day scheduled for the attack, the *Jeffersonian* reported its suspicions of an impending battle in its weekly news.

RICHARD BONNYCASTLE

Miniature portrait of Colonel Sir Richard Bonnycastle.

Lieutenant Colonel Richard Henry Bonnycastle was Bill Johnston's second biggest obstacle to success (Van Rensselaer being number one). By the rebellion's start, Bonnycastle, forty-five, was a brevet major in the Royal Engineers and a lieutenant colonel in the militia.

He became a lieutenant before his eighteenth birthday. He served in the Napoleonic War and the War of 1812. He married Frances Johnston in 1812. They had twelve children in a twenty-year period.

In 1818, he published his first book, a history of Spanish America. He was posted to Toronto in 1832 and established himself as an arts patron and higher education advocate. People spoke of his gifts for geology and astronomy.

In 1837, he arrived in Kingston to complete construction of the new Fort Henry. As a militia colonel, he found himself "the senior officer capable of duty" and the de facto fort commandant when the Upper Canada rebellion began.

From his network of informants, Bonnycastle learned of Johnston's plot to station hundreds of rebel farmers in local inns and public houses. He wrote, "I took a strong guard of militia, visited every suspected house before midnight, and, upon pain of death, forbade the inmates to leave their abodes."

Bonnycastle also knew which man Johnston had planted inside the fort to sabotage the cannons and blow up the magazines. Bonnycastle confronted him and received a confession. He ordered him from Canada, saying that if he returned, "no mercy should be shown to him." Bonnycastle did not arrest the man because he was "unwilling to dampen the ardor of the brave militia who garrisoned the fort, or to frighten the townspeople by stories of blowing up magazines."

Bonnycastle called up militia units along Lake Ontario and the St. Lawrence River. He requested and received a force of Mohawks from the nearby reservation to patrol the lakeshore and to defend Gananoque. He had men cut irregular holes in the ice near Kingston to foil an assault by sleigh. He barricaded Kingston with the help of a group of lumbermen, who tore apart a timber raft to build a breastwork on the waterfront.

Bonnycastle sent scouts to the United States to spy on the Patriots, and he set up a series of signal rockets to warn of an approaching enemy. He knew the Patriots' plans for Gananoque, but he believed a second army intended to cross the frozen lake and attack Kingston from the west. He dispatched defenders to intercept them. (No such attack occurred, nor is there evidence that the Patriots planned one.)

Rebels Move on Hickory Island

When Barnett stopped briefly in Clayton on February 21, 1838, she saw a town teeming with armed men and horse-drawn sleighs at the ready. A significant force of Americans milled in the chilly streets. Heustis reported that six hundred men waited for the order to march that day.

Martin Woodruff, forty, the sheriff of Onondaga County and a colonel in the New York State militia, brought a company of men. So did Lyman Leach, forty, a neighbor of Woodruff from Salina, New York.

Oblivious to Bonnycastle's preparations for them, the Patriots prepared to move out. That evening, fortified with brandy, General Van Rensselaer led fifty men across the ice and occupied Hickory Island and its one small dwelling. The eighty-acre wooded island lies inside the Canadian border, four miles west of Clayton and eight miles south of Gananoque.

The next morning, Captain Heustis and Captain Leach led fifty men each to the island. Colonel Woodruff stayed in Clayton to direct men to the island as new volunteers arrived.

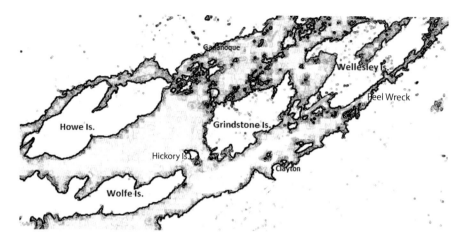

Bill Johnston's playground showing Hickory Island and the site of the *Peel* raid.

The intent was to use the island as an assembly point for the raid on Gananoque. But Hickory Island became a repeat of Navy Island. Van Rensselaer dithered and drank. Volunteers lost interest. According to Heustis, "A large number of men in sleighs visited the island during the day, but many of them only stopped a short time. At no time did our force consist of more than 300 men."

The winter cold (Bonnycastle noted in his book that the temperature was twenty-seven degrees below zero that night), boredom and distrust of Van Rensselaer wore down the Patriots. They drifted home in groups. Late that afternoon, the general also abandoned the island. Heustis held out, as he chronicled:

> *About sundown Bill Johnston joined us. Our number had then materially diminished. There was much disappointment manifested at not finding a larger force assembled. We had calculated on a thousand men, good and true, for this expedition, and had provided an ample supply of arms, ammunition, and provisions. With feelings of deep mortification, we were obliged to pronounce the enterprise a failure. But so unwilling was I to relinquish the attack that I still offered to go if 99 would accompany me in the hazardous assault. My proposal was considered too daring and impolitic, and but few were willing to embark in an expedition which promised nothing but inevitable defeat and destruction. We therefore returned to French Creek, Johnston and myself being the last to leave the island.*

Bonnycastle sent cavalry, artillery, infantry and militia units to confront the invaders on the evening of the twenty-second. They reached the island before dawn the next day and captured two men. The *Jeffersonian* reported that the men, John Packard and George Hulsenberg from Clayton, had no connection to the Patriots and had gone to Hickory Island out of curiosity. The colony imprisoned them for six months.

During the Texas Revolution two years earlier, the Andrew Jackson government did not enforce the Neutrality Act and may have aided the American participants. Under Martin Van Buren (elected in 1836 and formerly Jackson's vice president), Patriots and Hunters soon learned that the government refused to treat them like their Texas revolutionary brethren. Instead, the U.S. military confiscated arms and arrested violators.

Bonnycastle also arrested fifty Midland farmers found marching on Kingston in league with Johnston.

Van Rensselaer blamed Mackenzie for the Hickory Island failure, saying the latter had interfered with his plans. Mackenzie had nothing to do with it. Every participant in the aborted raid knew the truth, which the *Jeffersonian* put into print in its next weekly edition:

> *A number of the Patriots under the command of Mr. Van No General, congregated on Hickory Island in the St. Lawrence Thursday of last week, for the alleged purpose of visiting Canada, but owing as is alleged to the stupidity, cowardice, drunkenness or some other trait in the said Van Rensselaer, the Patriots dispersed.*

In the following days, U.S. marshals arrested Heustis, Johnston, Woodruff and Van Rensselaer for breaching the Neutrality Act. All four raised bail. Johnston and Van Rensselaer eventually served time for the Hickory Island attack.

Following the Hickory Island embarrassment, colonial Canada's greatest unwitting ally, Van Rensselaer, faded from view and never commanded a Patriot force again.

6

New Rebel Alliance Formed

March 1838

Two months after Donald McLeod marched off to invade Canada near Detroit, he limped back from a resounding defeat. At one point, he had disguised himself as a woman in a vain attempt to avoid arrest by the U.S. army as it enforced the Neutrality Act. At trial, a sympathetic jury acquitted him. (Throughout the rebellion, American juries tended toward extreme leniency when it came to convicting rebels.)

On March 19, 1838, McLeod joined Dr. Charles Duncombe, Silas Fletcher, Samuel Chandler and other Canadian Patriot leaders in Lockport, New York (twelve miles east of Niagara Falls). They formed the Canadian Refugee Relief Association (CRRA).

On the surface, it mimicked a philanthropic organization designed to help displaced Canadians. In reality, its mission was to raise funds for continued warfare against Britain's colonies. Dr. Alexander Mackenzie, a rebel refugee from Hamilton, Upper Canada, became the first CRRA president. General McLeod took on an unofficial role as military operative and organizer of satellite committees.

William Lyon Mackenzie, though a CRRA executive committee member, did not attend the inaugural meeting and played a minor and diminishing role in it. Mackenzie had begun to disavow violence as a means to achieve reform. The committee's members did nothing to encourage him to stay involved, partly because they didn't trust him. As historian John Charles Dent put it, "His discretion was not to be depended upon"; that is, he was a blabbermouth. Patriot leaders finally realized that secrecy was an important ingredient to success.

INCOGNITO EX-GOVERNOR OUTTED

The only incident in the Patriot War that may elicit a smile occurred in Watertown, New York, late in March 1838.

Both loyalists and rebels blamed Sir Francis Bond Head for causing the 1837 Upper Canada rebellion. Dr. Egerton Ryerson, a respected minister, author, educator and loyalist, wrote to a friend, saying, "The fact is however, that Sir Francis Head deserves impeachment just as much as Samuel Lount deserves execution. Morally speaking, I cannot but regard Sir Francis as the more guilty culprit of the two."

On March 23, 1838, the Colonial Office in London, which so far had ignored angry delegations from Upper Canada, reacted to the rebellion by replacing the incompetent Bond Head with hard-hearted Sir George Arthur, fifty-three.

To avoid his enemies real and imagined, Bond Head decided to travel incognito home to England through America. In late March, he departed for New York accompanied by his friend Judge Jonas Jones, forty-five, a member of the Family Compact's inner circle. Hoping to slip away unnoticed, Bond Head disguised himself as Jones's servant.

They crossed from Kingston to New York State in a small boat and then traveled to Watertown, New York, in a hired wagon. The driver dropped them off at a hotel in central Watertown. That hotel, owned by Luther Gibson, was then the Canadian Patriots' local hangout. Men recognized and surrounded Jones—reports state he resembled a fox cornered by hounds—and regaled him with their political opinions. His servant quietly slipped away.

Hugh Scanlan, twenty-seven, a friend and confidant of Bill Johnston and a Patriot veteran of the Hickory Island raid, mingled with the Patriots that day. He noted the servant's long absence and set out to find him. He encountered Bond Head lounging in a wheelbarrow in a nearby stable and recognized him.

Months earlier, William Lyon Mackenzie had pledged £500 for the capture of Bond Head. Scanlan and his Patriot buddies knew about the reward. So did Sir Francis.

Scanlan promised the ex-governor that he wouldn't be harmed and offered to introduce him to the lads. So it came to pass that a clutch of so-called murderous traitors treated their captives—two principal elites of the notorious Family Compact—to the best fare the hotel had to offer. That afternoon, Bond Head and Jones rode out to rousing cheers from the expatriate Canadians.

As for Mackenzie's big reward for Bond Head, everyone knew the diminutive firebrand didn't have five cents to his name.

7

First Patriots Executed

April 1838

Not all of William Lyon Mackenzie's rebel officers succeeded in escaping to the United States following their defeat at Montgomery's Tavern in December 1837. Authorities captured Samuel Lount, Peter Matthews and Anthony Van Egmond, plus numerous enlisted men.

Van Egmond, sixty-two, originally from the Netherlands, became ill in prison and died in a hospital four weeks after his arrest, probably from pneumonia.

Peter Matthews, fifty-one, was the son of an infantry captain who fought on the British side in the Revolutionary War and settled in Upper Canada after independence. Matthews enlisted during the War of 1812, became a sergeant and fought in various campaigns for Canada. He was a respected and prosperous farmer and a leading local figure. Peter married twice and had eight children from his two marriages. In Mackenzie's ill-fated army, Peter served as a captain.

Samuel Lount, forty-six, was born in Catawissa, Pennsylvania. He came to Upper Canada in 1811 with his parents and settled in Whitchurch Township northeast of Toronto. In 1815, he married Elizabeth Soules, and they had seven children. He became a blacksmith and moved his family to Holland Landing, north of Toronto, in 1818. He prospered financially and developed a reputation as a man to count on if you needed help. Lount was a member of a pacifist Quaker sect called the Children of Peace.

In 1834, Lount won a seat in the colonial assembly and fought for political reform alongside Mackenzie. In December 1837, he and other Children of Peace members forsook a life of pacifist teachings and joined the rebel attack on Toronto. (Two died at the initial skirmish.)

Sketch of Charles Durand.

Peter Matthews, one of the first Patriots to hang.

Lount's 1837 arrest notice—offering £500 for his capture—described him as a slow talker, six feet tall or more, with a long face, sallow complexion, dark eyebrows and black hair with gray flecks.

The new lieutenant governor of Upper Canada, Sir George Arthur, former lieutenant governor of Van Diemen's Land (now Tasmania) and its penal colony, immediately decided to make examples of convicted rebel leaders. He condemned Lount and Matthews to death. Lount's wife wrote letters pleading for mercy and once begged Sir George on her knees to spare her husband. Sir George ignored her and petitions signed by a reported eight thousand people (some sources say thirty thousand) asking for mercy.

In his memoirs, Heustis recalled details of the last days of Matthews and Lount that he received from another prisoner, Charles Durand, twenty-six. (Like many of the 885 people arrested in Upper Canada, Durand's only crime was associating with reformers.):

Matthews always bore up in spirits well. He was, until death, firm in his opinion of the justice of the cause he had espoused. He never recanted. He was ironed and kept in the darkest cell in the prison, like a murderer. He slept sometimes in blankets that were wet and frozen. He had nothing to cheer him but the approbation of his companions and his conscience.

Lount was ironed, though kept in a better room. He used to tell us often, in writing, not to be downcast; that he believed "Canada would yet be free," and that we were "contending in a good cause." He said he was not sorry for what he had done, and that he would do so again. This was his mind until death.

Lount was a social and excellent companion, and a well-informed man. He sometimes spoke to us under the sill of our door. He did so on the morning of his execution! He bid us "farewell!" and said he was on his way to another world. He was calm.

The gallows was erected just before our window grates. We could see all plainly. The martyrs ascended the platform with unfaltering steps, like men. Lount turned his head to his friends, as if to say a "long farewell!" He and Matthews knelt and prayed, and were then launched into eternity. O! the horror of our feelings! Who can describe our emotions!

The reference to Lount's writing likely refers to how captives exchanged notes by rolling them into tubes and shoving them through small-diameter holes in the prison walls. Durand called this the "paper telegraph."

Lount and Matthews died by hanging outside the Toronto jail on April 12, 1838, before a large crowd. Lount's last words were: "Be of good courage boys, I am not ashamed of anything I've done, I trust in God, and I'm going to die like a man." Today, those words appear on a historical plaque at King and Toronto Streets, near the site of Toronto's old jail.

Spectators witnessed more barbarity than they bargained for that day. An overly long drop in the gallows nearly tore Lount's head from his body. His blood spewed on his clothes and puddled the ground. One Rochester paper reported, "Two ruffians seized the end of the rope and dragged the mangled corpse [of

On November 28, 1859, twenty-one years later, William Lyon Mackenzie removed the bodies and reburied them in the Toronto Necropolis. He was accompanied by Samuel Lount's brother George, Samuel's son Charles and Samuel's nephew William.

Lount] along the ground into the jail yard, someone exclaiming this is the way every damned rebel deserves to be used."

The jailors refused to give the bodies of Lount and Matthews to their families and buried them in Toronto's potter's field near the present-day intersection of Bloor and Yonge Streets. Lount and Matthews became the first rebel leaders to die by hanging, but far from the last.

JAILBREAK PLANNED

Image of Linus Miller.

From Lockport, New York, General Donald McLeod followed the countdown to the execution of Lount and Matthews with sorrow and probably frustration. Given the mass of militia in Toronto, any attempt to free them by force would surely fail.

Instead, McLeod focused his attention on the Hamilton jail. It held six rebels, part of Dr. Duncombe's army, scheduled for execution on April 20. McLeod knew he could raise a raiding party on short notice. Plenty of men on both sides of the border stood ready to answer his call. All he lacked was a mission head. From the ranks of eager young men, a natural leader emerged.

Linus Wilson Miller was a wildly idealistic American drawn into the campaign to liberate Canada. He grew up on a farm near Stockton, New York, but abandoned the agrarian world to study law. At age twenty, the Patriot War diverted his career—for eight years.

The rants by William Lyon Mackenzie and Patriot leaders about Family Compact depredations in Upper Canada struck a nerve in Miller. In the spring of 1838, he toured the Niagara region of Upper Canada to see firsthand the suffering of Canadians. During his visit, he said he found "a large majority of the most respectable Canadians" willing to describe the "blight and mildew of misrule" that changed loyal subjects into enemies of the Crown. He was hooked.

He later described his Patriot War experiences in a book crammed with idealism and dashes of American jingoism, such as:

> [Canadians] *turned their eyes to the United States, studied our glorious and peaceful institutions, until they imbibed the spirit of the heroes of the American Revolution, and felt the God-like divinity of liberty stirring within their souls.*

In the common vernacular, he was way over the top, but it demonstrates the heightened passion of young Americans of that era.

On April 14, 1838, two days after the executions of Lount and Matthews, Miller attended a CRRA executive council meeting in Lockport with CRRA president, Dr. Alexander Mackenzie and General McLeod. McLeod asked Miller to lead the raid on the Hamilton jail, and he accepted.

According to his memoirs, Miller crossed into Canada and raised two hundred men from within the local populace. He sent one small group to attack Hamilton's Dundern Castle as a diversion. He sent others to commandeer a steamer in Hamilton's port for their escape. He planned to lead a third party to storm the jail and hustle the prisoners to the steamer.

He made his way to Hamilton in wintry weather, only to discover armed men guarding the castle, the port and the jail. He accused Jacob Beemer, twenty-four, a member of his raiding party and a veteran of Dr. Duncombe's uprising, of tipping off the British, though Miller had scant evidence. The real reason his plan failed had more to do with intelligence gathering by the Upper Canada military. Spies reported a possible Patriot assault scheduled for July 4, and Colonel Allan MacNab had already placed the militia on high alert.

Luckily, local contacts told Miller the government had reprieved the death sentences. He canceled the jail break, dispersed the two hundred volunteers and hurried home. He narrowly avoided capture when he stopped at a store to buy supplies:

> *I repaired to the store of the Mills brothers, one of whom was at Lockport as a refugee. About 3 o'clock, PM, Sir Allan MacNab, commander of the forces, Colonel Lang, Judge Jones, the magistrates of the town, and a large number of other gentlemen, came into the store, and, without ceremony, commenced scrutinizing my person. Not a word was spoken, but all gazed eagerly upon my countenance, as if expecting there to read the information they were in quest of.*

Miller nonchalantly continued shopping. After twenty minutes, MacNab, Jones and their party departed but posted two police officers outside the door:

> *Turning to Mr. Mills, I said, "If you are ready, Sir, I will close my business with you." "Certainly," said he, "step into the counting room." This room was at the opposite end of the store. He followed me, closing the door of the room after him. In five minutes I had altered my disguise, passed through a trap door into the cellar, and from thence into a back street. Before, however, I had got twenty rods from the store, upon looking round, I saw a company of soldiers surrounding it, and the whole posse of my late visitors entering the door.*

Miller returned to New York without further incident. It would not be his last trip to Upper Canada or his last complaint concerning Jacob Beemer.

8

Secret Society Forms to Plan Invasions

May 1838

Following a major Patriote defeat in February 1838, the military chief, Robert Nelson, knew victory was impossible if he continued to publicly recruit and train his army. Government spies and informers attended every public meeting. So he created a secret society to build his army and raise funds. Word of his initiative found its way to the

Multiple sources suggest the Hunters Lodge took its name from Dr. James Hunter, forty-eight, a Canadian Patriot who marched with William Lyon Mackenzie. The similarity is a trite coincidence. The name came from Nelson's group, *Frères-Chasseurs*, which translates into "hunter brothers" or "hunter brotherhood."

English Canadian rebels. In April, General Donald McLeod journeyed to Vermont to investigate. He liked what he saw.

In May 1838, McLeod and other rebel leaders created a secret society called the Hunters Lodge, or Patriot Hunters. Grand lodges appeared first in St. Albans, Vermont; followed by Cleveland, Ohio (the western headquarters); and Rochester, New York (the eastern headquarters).

MEMBERSHIP SOARS

This symbol of the Hunters Lodge, the American eagle carrying away the British lion, appeared on Hunter proclamations.

Fascination with the Hunters caught hold and spread through the border towns like fire in dry grass. With great fanfare, new lodges opened weekly across the northeastern United States. In Watertown, New York, Daniel Heustis helped start a local lodge in May that quickly drew 1,900 members, including Bill Johnston.

By the summer's end, Hunters had set up hundreds of lodges in America. They ranged from Maine to Wisconsin and as far inland as Kentucky. At their height, the Hunters claimed 200,000 members, though 40,000 is probably more accurate. Hunter cells also formed on the Canadian side, but secretly.

Hunters held four degrees of membership: snowshoe, beaver, master hunter and patriot hunter. Members were initiated as snowshoes and learned new secret signs and passwords at each stage. Recruits recited secret oaths on their knees, blindfolded, with knives pointed at their throats. Betrayal of lodge secrets meant death. A member's house could be burned for disobeying orders.

Senior Hunter leaders tended to also be Masons. That affiliation cemented their positions in the new brotherhood and gave them ample experience with oaths, secret rituals and related arcana.

While the Hunter leaders bragged that they had twenty-five thousand armed men ready to fight, few had any interest in war. Hunter membership became the best way to make economic and political connections in difficult times. The depression and ongoing banking crises gripping the U.S. border states united the diverse classes. Politicians, merchants, businessmen, mechanics, farmers and common laborers signed up.

Motivations varied. For many, the Hunters movement was an altruistic attempt to give Canada a republican government. Others foresaw a chance to make money. Profiteers, land speculators and carpetbaggers mixed with the honest idealists.

The undeclared Patriot War also provided an opportunity for Americans to complete unfinished business from the Revolutionary War: to rid the continent of monarchists and possibly extend the U.S. border northward.

The Hunters' stunning growth soon overpowered allied associations and, as a side effect, united them. The Hunters stole members from Mackenzie's Patriots, McLeod's Canadian Refugee Relief Association and the Sons of Liberty, another secret society formed by Patriot general Henry S. Handy in Michigan.

JOHNSTON AND MCLEOD PLOT REVENGE

For much of William Johnston's life, residents on both St. Lawrence River shores either revered or hated him. His uncompromising belief in fighting injustice, combined with his intimate knowledge of the Thousand Islands' secrets, allowed Johnston to change the course of armed conflicts and ignore laws with near impunity.

Bill Johnston's signature event—the one that earned him the moniker "Pirate Bill"—occurred early on the rainy morning of May 30, 1838.

Shortly after midnight, Johnston and at least twenty-one armed men, crudely disguised as Indians, started shadowing the *Sir Robert Peel* in two rowboats as the steamer made its way up the American Channel beside Wellesley Island. When the ship stopped to take on a load of firewood (fuel for its boilers), Johnston's men landed downstream and began to skulk the dark forest toward the *Peel*.

With Johnston that night was his co-conspirator, Donald McLeod. Ostensibly, they planned to capture the *Peel* and use it as troop ship for a series of attacks on Canada by Patriots and Hunters gathering in the border states. In reality, their actions that night were part war strategy and part revenge.

Johnston's motives for reprisal stemmed from heavy-handed English justice twenty-five years earlier during the War of 1812. The *Caroline*'s destruction in December 1837 had enraged him and rekindled his war with Britain.

Five months after McLeod's flight from Upper Canada mobs, his wife and sons escaped to Ogdensburg, New York, penniless and hungry. In a letter sent in May 1838 to a friend, McLeod promised retaliation:

> *I would have written to you before now, but on my arrival at Ogdensburg, I found my wife and family in a state of complete destitution. The infernal hell-bound, god-forsaken Tories stripped her and the children of every farthing's worth in the world—did not leave a second shift to her back, nor a second shirt to the boys. Oh God! when I embraced her in my arms, she was a living skeleton. Oh Great Jehovah!!! I could not weep—but the feelings of my heart and the throbbing of my breast may be conceived but cannot be described. Never mind, I will have revenge, yes, ample revenge.*

For Johnston and McLeod, the attack on the *Peel* went beyond their Patriot duty. It was personal.

Johnston's hand-picked pirate crew included a mixed bag of fellow smugglers, common bandits (part of a contingent of white trash living in the then isolated Thousand Islands) and politically motivated rebels. Two of the latter were Marshall Forward and Samuel Frey.

MARSHALL FORWARD

Marshall W. Forward was born in Bath, Upper Canada, in 1817. Living in the hometown of Bill Johnston, Forward likely heard many tales, true and exaggerated, about Johnston (by then living in America). In 1837, Forward moved to Watertown, New York. Like many young men in 1838, he was stirred by the Patriot cause and fell in league with Bill Johnston. Following his arrest for the *Peel* raid, he remained in jail until mid-December 1838 awaiting a trial that never happened.

SAMUEL FREY

Born (1799), raised and married in Fulton County, New York, Samuel Challott Frey moved to the village of Philadelphia, Jefferson County, in the mid-1820s. In the mid-1830s, he relocated his family to Brockville, Upper Canada, where he set up a wholesale and retail jewelry business. Being a vocal reformer, he had to flee from Tory gangs to America after the Upper Canada rebellion started. He joined the Patriots and was a junior officer during the Hickory Island occupation in February 1838.

Immediately following the *Peel* raid, he fled New York State as fast as possible. Identified by another Canadian refugee, who was likely after the $250 reward for Frey's capture, a sheriff jailed him in Canton, Ohio. A mob of Patriots and sympathizers assembled in the streets and threatened to lynch any snitch working for the prosecution. At Frey's trial, no witnesses came forth, and the judge released him.

A year later, Frey sent a letter to William Lyon Mackenzie (dated September 6, 1839) from Canton. The bulk of it described local politics, and he said that he and his family fared well. He added, "I wish Wm. Johnston would come this way. Tell him so, if you see him."

PIRATES LOST IN FOREST

On the way to the *Peel*, at least nine of Bill Johnston's crew got lost in the dark, wet forest. Besides Johnston and McLeod, eleven men gathered near the wharf and studied the steamer in the glow of its lamps: Hugh Scanlan, Samuel Frey, William Anderson, James Potts, Marshall Forward, William Nicholls, William Smith, brothers Chester and Seth Warner, Nathan Lee and Henry Hunter. (We know this from eyewitness accounts.)

The year-old, 160-foot-long passenger steamer belonged to prominent members of the Family Compact, including Judge Jonas Jones. It carried approximately a dozen first-class passengers—members or associates of the colony's governing elite. In one stateroom, Ella Sampson, wife of Kingston's mayor, her daughter Madeline and a friend prepared for bed. In another stateroom, two well-connected militia officers talked over liquor and cigars with three businessmen. Colonel Richard Bullock Jr., forty-five, served as adjutant general of the Upper Canada militia. Colonel Richard Duncan Fraser, fifty-

Ella Sampson dropped a silk apron as she fled. Bill added it to his loot and gave it to his daughter, Kate. The Thousand Islands Museum in Clayton, New York, has part of that apron on display.

four, held the patronage job of collector of customs in Brockville and commanded a militia regiment.

Deciding not to wait for his lost men, Johnston ordered the charge. Letting out war whoops, the thirteen raiders raced across a clearing and up the gangplank. Within a half hour, they had hustled the eighty-five sleepy passengers and crew at gunpoint to the wharf. Except for one fistfight, where Colonels Bullock and Fraser tried to better the pirates, the affray resulted in no injuries.

Johnston's gang robbed every person and ransacked all cabins for valuables. Colonel Fraser lost £300 in bank notes. The businessmen carried a combined amount of £1,100. The purser held £400 in ship's funds and over £6,000 being sent to Toronto to pay troops. Passengers gave up jewelry, articles of silver and silk apparel.

Johnston ordered the ship untied, and it drifted downstream. Johnston later told historian Franklin Hough that "a Cleveland committee" had promised to send 150 men to help run the *Peel* and to capture the *Great Britain*, an even larger steamer. Whether the promise of men was true or not, no one showed up. Since none of Johnston's men (of those not lost in the woods) could restart the ship's boilers, he ordered them to burn it. With cries of "Remember the *Caroline*," they set it aflame and retreated in their boats.

Fire engulfed its wooden decks, cabins and hull. The flaming hulk drifted downstream and grounded on a rocky islet. Consumed to the waterline, it capsized and sank. The islet is still known as Peel Island.

At dawn, another steamer took the stranded passengers to Kingston. They claimed that a large contingent of ruffians had attacked them—the truth being too embarrassing to tell. For example, Colonel Fraser estimated that fifty men boarded the *Peel* with one hundred men in reserve.

Johnston and his crew retired to their Abel's Island hideout (now called Picton Island), where the lost raiders joined them. Over breakfast, Johnston distributed the looted valuables and money among trusted operatives for safekeeping. He gave Scanlan the troop wages, displaying a massive level of trust. (It is likely that Scanlan was one of Johnston's tea-smuggling crew in the years before the Patriot War.) As the day wore on, the raiders drifted away—eleven into the law's shackles.

Sketch of Peel Island by Benson Lossing from his *Pictorial Field-Book of the War of 1812*, 1869.

The *Peel's* destruction set off a massive manhunt for Johnston. For months, he was the most wanted man on both sides of the border. The British and American governments each mobilized a small armada and army to find him. Pirate Bill hid in the largely unpopulated Thousand Islands maze, an archipelago no one knew better than he.

9

Rogue Patriots Attack at Short Hills

June 1838

On June 10, 1838, twenty-six Patriot raiders assembled beside the Niagara River in New York State. With Canadian liberation as their goal and deluded by a promise that thousands of Canadians would rise up to join them in armed revolt, they crossed into Upper Canada to strike an undefined blow for the Patriot cause.

The eighteen Canadians and eight Americans elected their officers. James Morreau (or Morrow), thirty-two, a tanner from Pennsylvania, became leader. Samuel Chandler, forty-seven, became commissary. Benjamin Wait, twenty-four, became a major. Jacob Beemer, twenty-eight, a carpenter, and Alexander McLeod, twenty-four, a farmer, became captains.

Benjamin Wait was born in the colony to American immigrant parents. In 1837, he lived west of Niagara Falls, employed as a businessman and schoolteacher. When the Upper Canada rebellion ignited in Toronto in December 1837, Wait joined Dr. Charles Duncombe's uprising near London just as the British dispersed the rebels. He fled to the United States, crossing the Niagara River by canoe. He joined William Lyon Mackenzie's army in the occupation of Navy Island with the rank of lieutenant.

Morreau's company crossed the Niagara River at Grand Island and hiked stealthily through ravines and forests to a place called Short Hills near St. Catharine's. They set up camp and sent word to Patriot general Donald McLeod that they awaited his orders to attack something. Unseen for over a week, they waited for a reply. Local farmers welcomed them into their homes, and a dozen joined the marauders.

Benjamin Wait, from the cover of his 1843 memoirs.

During that interlude, Morreau circulated a proclamation designed to stir up local support:

> *Canadians: We have at last been successful in planting the standard of liberty in one part of our oppressed country. Canadians! Come to our*

assistance as you prize property, happiness and life; Come to our assistance.
Canadians! This is the hour of your redemption. Rally to the standard of
the Free and the tyranny of England will cease to exist in our land. We
pledge safety of property and life to all who do not opposed us; but resistance
shall be met by men who are determined to conquer or die.

The last thing Donald McLeod wanted was a rogue invasion. The CRRA and other Patriot organizations planned a major offensive for July 4, and he didn't want anyone prematurely antagonizing the colony. McLeod called on Linus Miller—now his aide-de-camp with the rank of colonel—to find Morreau and relay a simple command: cease hostilities and return immediately.

Colonel Miller crossed into Canada. With him was James Waggoner, thirty-eight, a former Canadian living in Lewistown, New York, and a well-armed eighteen-year-old saddle maker from Pennsylvania calling himself David Deal, a young man with a secret. They soon found Morreau's gang.

In his memoirs, Miller wrote that Morreau told him he had joined the raid because he was promised three thousand local fighters. A mere dozen had joined. Morreau urged his men, now over forty in number, to follow General McLeod's orders and retreat. The men debated the order and voted to stay and fight. Morreau promptly resigned his command.

According to Miller, Jacob Beemer then took over leadership. His first order of business was plunder. After sundown on June 21, Beemer led a band of men to rob a home simply because the occupants were English loyalists. They next traveled to the town of St. Johns and confronted a troop of lancers (cavalry) staying at a tavern owned by William Osterhout, an ardent loyalist. Miller and Morreau joined them to, as Miller wrote, "prevent what mischief we could."

Led by Beemer, the Patriots besieged the tavern and traded shots with the barricaded lancers for half an hour in the dark night. The exchange wounded one lancer and two rebels. The rebels piled straw next to the tavern and threatened to set it aflame. The lancers surrendered and marched at gunpoint into the forest.

At the urging of Beemer and Chandler, the rebels slung seven ropes over tree branches and selected seven lancers for execution—revenge for the hanging of Samuel Lount and Peter Matthews that April.

Miller, Morreau and Wait persuaded the raiders to be merciful. At Miller's bidding, the lancers swore an oath never to use force against Patriots. When the lancers gave their word, he released them. The lancers promptly reported their capture. (They also described how Miller had saved them from hanging.)

Army units rushed into the Short Hills area. The Patriot raiders broke and ran for the border. Few made it. Redcoats captured thirty-eight raiders and sympathizers—including Miller, Morreau, Wait, Chandler and Beemer—and hauled them to Hamilton's jail to await trial.

Once captured, Deal told Miller his real name, William Reynolds, and confessed that he had helped Bill Johnston destroy the *Sir Robert Peel*. Reynolds confided that he was terrified the English might learn his secret and hang him for it, perhaps unaware that raiding Upper Canada was also a hanging offense.

Peel Pirates Arrested and Tried

Within days of the *Sir Robert Peel* raid, American constables arrested thirteen of Johnston's pirate crew—including men who had never set foot on the ship: William Anderson, Marshall Forward, William Nicholls, James Potts, Hugh Scanlan, William Smith, Chester and Seth Warner, Nathan Lee, Henry Hunter, Jesse Thayer, James Hunter and William Lester. The constables also recovered any stolen loot in the prisoners' possession.

Inexplicably, the court granted Scanlan bail. He promptly disappeared from the theater of the Patriot War.

New York governor William Learned Marcy posted a reward of $500 for Bill Johnston's capture, and $250 for Daniel McLeod, Samuel Frey and Robert Smith. Other men identified as participants included William Coopernoll (arrested by Captain William Vaughan in December 1838), William Robbins, John Farrow and John Tarr.

Various authorities connected Lyman Leach, William Reynolds and Russell Phelps to the *Peel* raid, but their names are not on the official list of twenty-one men arrested or wanted. All raiders on the *Peel* were identified by passengers and crew. If involved, these three were in the group lost in the woods.

People in Jefferson County, New York, where most *Peel* raiders resided, didn't condone piracy but supported Johnston's men. The county waited expectantly for the *Peel* trials to start. The show opened on June 22, 1838, at the county courthouse in Watertown. And what a spectacle!

Wanting to prove that the United States didn't condone attacks on British property, American authorities sent the A-team to the trial, including

Governor William Marcy and the state attorney general, Samuel Beardsley. The *Peel* captain, Captain John Armstrong, attended as a witness, as did the ship's purser and several *Peel* passengers.

Judge John Cushman read a long list of indictments against each accused. The court put William Anderson, a Canadian from Bill Johnston's hometown of Bath, on the stand first. Bernard Bagley, forty-six, a Watertown lawyer and friend of Bill Johnston, defended Anderson pro bono.

Over the next six days, witness after witness testified to Anderson's activities before and during the *Peel* raid and proved his association with Bill Johnston.

One *Peel* pirate, Nathan Lee, became a state witness in exchange for immunity from prosecution. Bagley and his partners produced a stream of people who testified that Lee was a drunken, lying lowlife. The tactic worked—the court rejected Lee as a witness.

Bagley also asked for and received a court order prohibiting publication of evidence until the trial concluded. So the eager public subsisted on rumors.

On June 26, Beardsley addressed the jury with an impassioned speech lasting hours. He stressed how important the jury's decision was to the reputation of New York State and the nation.

After two hours of deliberation, the twelve men returned. The jury foreman announced the verdict to a hushed court: not guilty. Newspapers in Upper Canada spewed scathing criticism of American justice. U.S. newspapers reported the trial with little editorializing. William Lyon Mackenzie gloated in the pages of the *Gazette*, his U.S.-based newspaper.

The next day, the court arraigned Marshall Forward but put off his trial until the state prosecutor could gather more evidence. In the end, no other *Peel* raider faced a trial. With the lingering resentment against the monarchy, Jefferson County men were unlikely to convict any of them, and the prosecutor knew that. Within six months, the court released every accused man on his own recognizance.

While Bill Johnston's henchmen could return to their old lives, the government had different rules for the pirate boss. The hunt for him never stopped.

10

Rebels Win Off the Battlefield

July–August 1838

Of the fifty Midland farmers arrested in February 1838 by Lieutenant Colonel Richard Bonnycastle for plotting with Bill Johnston, nine faced charges under the British Treason Act (the rest being released). As ominous as a treason charge sounds, the act required two prosecution witnesses for a conviction, respected the defendant's right to legal representation and permitted defense counsel to examine prosecution's evidence in advance. In short, the accused received a fair trial for the standards of the time.

Portrait of a John A. Macdonald in his late twenties, 1842 or 1843. *Library and Archives Canada, C-004811.*

Eight defendants had the great fortune to hire a twenty-three-year-old, gangly, curly-haired barrister named John Alexander Macdonald to defend them.

Ahead of the trial, Macdonald rigorously challenged jurors. During the trial, he cast doubts on the validity of signed confessions and had them set aside. His cross-examinations caused prosecution witnesses to contradict one another, and he demonstrated the Crown's failure to prove intent.

The court tried Nelson Reynolds, said to be the leader, on July 4. Macdonald's legal tactics saw Reynolds acquitted on July 6. The prosecution dropped one case because evidence matched Reynolds's case. The trials of the six others resulted in acquittals.

Upper Canada newspapers ran the story and praised Macdonald's skill. That trial and others to follow built the foundation of Macdonald's legal career and a reputation that later served him well when he entered politics.

The Fox Bites the Hound

Following William Anderson's acquittal for arson, American authorities ignored other *Peel* raiders and committed troops and ships to prowl the Thousand Islands on the hunt for Bill Johnston. His henchmen simply went home or, as in the case of Donald McLeod, back to revolutionary business as usual.

Upper Canada had already committed significant military resources to catch the elusive pirate or his crew. The United States belatedly joined it.

At one point, British officers Lieutenant Colonel Henry Dundas, thirty-seven, and Captain Williams Sandom, fifty-three, met with U.S. Army general Alexander Macomb, fifty-six. They made a gentlemen's agreement to let each nation patrol the islands and waters of the other, but not the mainland, for Johnston or his gang. Anyone captured belonged to the country where apprehended. Citizens of Jefferson and St. Lawrence Counties took the sight of armed British ships anchored in U.S. harbors as an insult. Due to negative public opinion, the agreement did not last long.

Despite having a fleet from two nations combing the Thousand Islands, Johnston defied capture. Supplied with food and basic provisions by his family, Bill lived well. Catherine (always called Kate), eighteen, devoted herself to her father's welfare. Of all the Johnston clan, she most often rendezvoused with her father at his numerous hiding spots.

Bill's searchers began to follow his children, especially Kate, hoping she'd lead them to their quarry. A superb rower, a child of the islands and as cunning as her father, she flawlessly avoided navy patrols. For her efforts, the American press dubbed her "Queen of the Thousand Islands."

Throughout the summer of 1838, a combined force from two countries of five hundred men and at least four steamships, plus smaller boats, concerned themselves entirely with Johnston's capture. He drifted between the islands like mist at dawn, caring not which side of the border he roamed. A more cautious man would have stayed in U.S. waters. Whereas Johnston faced a jail term if captured by the Americans, a noose awaited him if caught by the British.

Lieutenant Colonel Richard Bonnycastle acknowledged Johnston's freedom of movement and ability to evade capture in his 1852 book, *Canada, As It Was, Is and May Be*:

Portrait of a young Kate Johnston.

> *Bill Johnson laughed at the efforts of the Governor and all the authorities. The Thousand Islands afforded him a secure retreat, and amongst their intricacies he hid his boats and his men. In vain, parties of sailors from Kingston examined them [the islands]; they were occasionally fired at by an unseen and vanishing enemy. The American Militia and Civil officers were equally unsuccessful, capturing about 250 pikes, but no pikemen.*

No man in Upper Canada wanted Johnston more than Lieutenant Colonel Bonnycastle. He saw catching and punishing Johnston as his duty. Bonnycastle had succeeded at every task and challenge in his career. The crafty river pirate stood in the way of his perfect record.

He ordered armed steamers to patrol the Thousand Islands' main passages and rowboats to poke into lesser channels for any evidence of Johnston. The effort met with some success:

> *I sent one of my adjutants…on a secret expedition to discover where the [Johnstons'] boats were concealed. The foe was off, but he found their bivouac on an almost inaccessible islet near the most narrow part of the*

Fiddler's Elbow is a narrow channel between two cliff-lined islands at the end of a wide St. Lawrence bay, north of Hill Island's western tip. The river sluices through it like water in the narrow end of a funnel. Eddies peel off from its precipitous shores, and currents boil off the bottom. The helmsman showed tremendous skill that night.

channels of the Thousand Isles at Fiddler's Elbow, and cleverly constructed inclined planes upon which these fast-rowing boats had been drawn up.

Bonnycastle hatched a plot to capture or destroy Johnston and his crew. One night, he loaded a company of militia onto a steamer in Kingston and ordered them to hide below deck. The next day, he set out on the pretext of visiting all military posts between Kingston and Prescott. His officers sauntered on the deck as a military band played. At night, lamps blazed. Bonnycastle used his ship as pirate bait.

Johnston obligingly took the bait, though not in the manner Bonnycastle expected.

On a moonlit night, Bonnycastle's side-wheeler churned upstream into Fiddler's Elbow on the return voyage. Unknown to him, Johnston had anchored two crude naval mines—watertight black powder kegs with flintlock detonators suspended from floats—in the channel's narrowest part. With the ship's bow a mere dozen yards before one mine, an officer spied a floating object and shouted a warning. The helmsman swerved the ship in the narrow channel and avoided both mines and the channel's deadly granite palisades. By daylight, the mines had vanished.

Bonnycastle's plot failed because Johnston knew it was a trap. A well-placed informant in Kingston had warned him of the men hidden below decks. Bonnycastle had a good idea who Johnston's informant was, though he never mentions him by name in his book. From then on, Bonnycastle's men monitored Johnston's spy day and night.

"Suffice it to observe," Bonnycastle wrote, "that the most interested party never stirred without my being acquainted with his motives; and that whenever we prepared to take the field, a false movement on his part would have instantly cost him his life, so well was he watched and guarded."

Short Hills Raiders Tried

Unlike the Midland farmers, whom courts tried in July 1838 under the Treason Act, the Patriots captured at Short Hills faced a Draconian new law. In January 1838, the Upper Canada government passed the Lawless Aggressions Act (that is a short version of the name) as a tool to defend itself against Patriot raids (in much the same way that modern countries passed anti-terrorism laws after September 11, 2001). The raiders captured at Short Hills were the first exposed to the new act.

An absolute abomination, the act permitted flimsy evidence from the prosecution and few avenues of defense for the accused. It applied to attacks by citizens of a country with which Great Britain was at peace and to British subjects who aided them.

The Upper Canada government brought the justice system's full weight and top brass to bear on the captured Short Hills raiders between July 18 and August 18, 1838. Lieutenant Colonel William Henry Draper, thirty-seven, the Upper Canada solicitor general, acted as prosecutor in several cases. On the bench, the accused faced Judge Jonas Jones, the Family Compact stalwart whom Patriots verbally abused in Watertown in March and who was part owner of the destroyed *Sir Robert Peel*. (Despite his obvious conflicts, the Family Compact allowed Jones to preside.)

In Miller's memoirs, he related an argument over law and procedure between himself, Judge Jones and Solicitor General Draper. Miller refused to plead guilty or not, stating that he had insufficient time to prepare a defense. His memoirs explain that he believed a plea would lead quickly to a death sentence.

Jones and Draper insisted repeatedly. Linus resisted. Jones flew into a rage twice and argued that Miller had the previous three weeks in jail to ready himself. Miller replied that he first heard the actual indictment against him minutes earlier and could therefore not have prepared in advance. Judge Jones, exasperated, offered Miller three days. He insisted on seven days and ultimately won his point.

As guards led Miller away, he passed James Morreau going into court. When asked to plead, Morreau obliged. The jury convicted him that day.

At Miller's eventual trial on August 1, the jury initially returned a verdict of guilty with a strong recommendation for mercy, according to Miller. Judge Jones told the jury that such a finding was virtually an acquittal. He sent the jury back, and it returned with the verdict unchanged. Jones lectured the jurymen on their duty and refused to accept the verdict. On the third occasion, the jury gave into Jones's diktat and dropped the request for mercy. That cleared the way for Jones to impose the death penalty, which he did on August 6.

Fortunately for the Short Hills raiders, they faced a civilian jury of which numerous men held reform sympathies, and mercy was possible. The court sentenced three men to prison for terms ranging from three to fourteen years, acquitted or released nineteen and condemned sixteen to death.

As the execution date neared, Lieutenant Governor Sir George Arthur grudgingly commuted fifteen sentences to transport for life in the Van Diemen's Land penal colony. They included Canadians Samuel Chandler, Benjamin Wait, Jacob Beemer, John Grant, John McNulty, James Gammell, Alexander McLeod, John Vernon and James Waggoner; and Americans Linus Miller, William Reynolds, Norman Mallory, David Taylor, George Cooley and Garret Van Camp.

Two women can take credit for the reprieves: Benjamin Wait's wife, Maria, and Samuel Chandler's daughter, Sarah. They petitioned and visited government leaders in Canada and the United States pleading for mercy. They warmed the heart of Lord Durham, the newly appointed governor general of the Canadian colonies. He urged Arthur to show restraint.

For one man—James Morreau, the original gang leader—even Lord Durham showed no mercy. Someone had to hang as a warning to others.

The court granted Morreau's final request that Linus Miller occupy his cell until the execution. Miller reported that Morreau, a Catholic, prayed night and day and seemed to reach a state of peace as his execution neared, even shedding tears of joy one night.

Morreau asked two priests in attendance the night before his execution to pass on a message:

> *My dying message to the world is, that I love the cause of liberty, for which I am about to suffer death, the better the nearer my end approaches; that my last days are spent in praying for its final triumph in Canada, and that I die in the full assurance of an eternity of bliss beyond the grave.*

On his way to the gallows the next day, Morreau said to Miller, "I die a martyr to a righteous cause, and I die happy. Death has no sting, for I shall soon wear a crown of glory."

On July 30, the district sheriff, Alexander Hamilton, forty-eight, led Morreau to the gallows. The usual hangman being unavailable, the sheriff offered $100 to anyone who would do the job. No one accepted, so Hamilton did the dirty deed himself, making sure the drop was sufficient to give Morreau a quick death. According to the local newspaper, the *Niagara Chronicle*, Morreau's lips moved in silent prayer as the trapdoor opened.

Upon hearing of Morreau's execution, Captain Daniel Heustis assembled fifty Hunters at Youngston, New York. He intended to cross the Niagara River at night, raid the Niagara jail and spirit the remaining Short Hills captives to safety. Hours before his expedition headed out, he learned the prisoners were shipped to Fort Henry.

JOHN MONTGOMERY ESCAPES

People believed that Fort Henry in Kingston, Upper Canada, was both impregnable and inescapable. In July 1838, a band of Patriot prisoners proved them wrong.

John Montgomery, fifty, was the son of loyalists who came to Canada following the U.S. Revolutionary War. A loyalist himself, he fought for Britain during the War of 1812. He served as county commissioner for roads and as a director of a mutual insurance company. He sympathized with the political reform movement in Upper Canada but disavowed armed conflict as a means to achieve

Photograph of John Montgomery (right) and fellow rebel John Anderson in 1875. Both escaped from Fort Henry in July 1838.

reform. He took no active role in the initial rebellion.

In 1837, Montgomery operated a tavern on Toronto's main route, Yonge Street, north of the city's border in those days. When William Lyon Mackenzie's rebel army assembled north of Toronto in early December 1837, they chose the tavern as their headquarters, and that was Montgomery's undoing.

Beyond this door at Fort Henry lies the trapdoor through which Patriot prisoners escaped in July 1838. *Photo by the author.*

The government force that routed the rebels on December 7 arrested Montgomery and burned his tavern. Despite his loyalist pedigree, the colony charged Montgomery with treason. The judge pronounced him guilty on flimsy evidence and sentenced him to death. The colony commuted that to transport for life to the penal colony in Tasmania. In May, the colony shipped Montgomery and fellow inmates from Toronto to Fort Henry on board the *Sir Robert Peel* (destroyed weeks later by Bill Johnston). The fort commander lodged Montgomery and fellow prisoners in a ground-level casement that normally served as troop barracks.

On Sunday, July 29, 1838, Montgomery and fourteen other Patriots participated in a great escape worthy of a movie. Montgomery detailed the breakout in a letter to William Lyon Mackenzie. Here is an abridged version:

We had learned that a portion of the wall in our room, although four and a half feet thick, had been completed only a short time, and the mortar was not yet dry.

Our sole implements of labor consisted of a piece of iron ten inches in length, and a disk nail. Having obtained half a cord of wood, we piled it up in the middle of the floor, as if for the purpose of airing our bed clothes, but in reality to hide the stone and mortar which we took from the hole. We, at length, went boldly to work; the unusual noise at first attracted the attention of the sentry, who came up to the window where I was reading the Bible, and asked the cause of it. I answered by pointing to two men who, apparently for their amusement, but in reality to deaden the strokes on the wall, were, with shovel and tongs, beating the stove with all their might, and eliciting thereby roars of laughter from their companions. We were not again interrupted.

We commenced on Tuesday and it was Sunday ere we had made a hole sufficiently large to enable us to get through. As the jail keeper had been married the Thursday before, we begged him to take his wife to church, and allow us to refrain from our usual airing. This he was very glad to do.

We then requested fourteen or fifteen pounds of biscuit, as we did not like the meat, and they kept better than bread; he sent four and a half pounds, all they had at the canteen.

Montgomery's escape route is regularly open to tourists at the fort. Through trapdoors in the last casement's floor, one descends a flight of steep steps into a damp, stone-lined tunnel with a low ceiling. (The escapees had a lantern to see their way.) Steps climb from the tunnel into linked rooms with carronades placed in front of closed gun ports. These guns are designed to fire into the fort's dry ditch if an enemy gets between the fort's inner and outer walls.

What Montgomery does not clearly explain is that once they escaped from the pit below the gun ports, they still needed to scale the outer dry ditch wall. The lowest point is fourteen feet high. They climbed it using a crude ladder made of boards.

We had hung up blankets, by permission of the keeper, to keep out the mosquitoes, and were thus enabled to complete our preparations without interruption. When the guard beat the evening tattoo and descended from the ramparts, we commenced our escape.

Behind this wall [in the next casement] *was an oak door leading to a subterranean passage which opened into a gun room; and as the shutters which covered the port holes hung on chains, we could easily let ourselves down by means of ropes made of our sheets into the sally port of a depth of ten feet; and by the same means were enabled to get on level ground.*

We reached the sally port in safety; but here I had the misfortune to fall into the pit and break my leg. One of my companions descended and took my hand, and we were pulled up by the rest.

It was a fearful night of storm and lightning, but we decided to take down towards the river, and when daylight came to take to the woods.

We had resolved to divide into parties for greater safety. We therefore divided our biscuits equally among fourteen men, [Stephen B.] *Brophy,* [Gilbert F.] *Morden,* [Walter] *Chase, and myself decided to make for Cape Vincent, agreeing to meet the others at Watertown, should we not be retaken.*

We traveled a considerable distance on Monday, and in the evening tried to get a boat. My leg having become greatly inflamed, and as I found it impossible to proceed, it was decided that we should rest in the woods and try, by application of cold water, to reduce the inflammation. This was done. At length, having got a boat, I was helped down to it, and about midnight we started in the direction of Kingston, and then crossed to Long Island, in order to escape a government vessel sent in search of us.

We landed on Long Island [now called Wolfe Island], *and pulled our boat up into the woods, but finding ourselves near people known to be unfriendly, we decided to cross the island and ascertain our chances of escape from the other side. We were obliged to carry our boat; which was very difficult to do with my broken leg, but I carried paddles and other articles. With great pain, and in a state of exhaustion, we at length succeeded in launching our boat and proceeded to what we felt sure was the*

Fort Henry escapees in July 1838 pulled the chain on a gun port, such as this, to enter the dry ditch. *Photo by the author.*

mainland. On arriving there we knelt down and thanked God for our safety, and earnestly prayed for that of our companions.

We soon found, however, that we were again on an island. Re-entering our boat almost famished, our slender provisions, two biscuits a day since leaving the fort, exhausted, we started for Cape Vincent, but were obliged to put ashore, being unable to manage the boat. We pulled her up and went to a house near the shore, and there learned that we were on American ground.

We asked a woman whom we saw there to get us a carriage to take us to Cape Vincent; but she refused, and sent to the field for her husband, who consented for $1.50 to take us in the boat. When I asked him if he had heard of the escape from the fort. He said, "Yes, that day at noon," adding, "I wish I knew where the poor fellows are, I would tell Bill Johnston and have them safe off before I sleep." When we told who we were, he earnestly requested us to take the money back. On landing threw up his hat and gave three cheers for the Patriots.

A crowd was soon collected, and I was relieved from the necessity of walking. Great sympathy and attention were shown us. A public dinner, largely attended, was given in our honor. On our arrival at Watertown, we were met by [John] Anderson and his party [the other escapees], and at length all joined us, save [Leonard] Watson and [John G.] Parker, who were retaken and put in heavy irons.

Being demanded by the British authorities, we were secreted until the opinion of the Governor of New York could be known. He decided that we should not be given up. While still suffering severely from the pain of my leg, I, a short time after arriving in Rochester, was knocked down by a large team and my skull fractured. I was for weeks unconscious, and it was a long time ere I recovered my usual health.

The other escapees, not named in Montgomery's report, were Edward Kennedy, Wilson Read, Thomas Tracy, Thomas Shepherd, Michael Shepherd, John Marr, John Stewart and William Stockdale. Some accounts state that the latter was recaptured.

The flight of the Fort Henry prisoners indirectly added to the growing legal reputation of John A. Macdonald. Lieutenant Colonel Henry Dundas, believing the fort inescapable, hastily arrested the jailer, John Ashley, for aiding the prisoners. Dundas exculpated Ashley when he learned the truth. Ashley, his reputation tarnished, hired Macdonald to sue Dundas for damages. Macdonald won the case and further respect for his skills.

John G. Parker

John Goldsworthy Parker was born in New Hampshire. As a young man, he and his younger brother, Reuben Alexander Parker, became traders in Sackets Harbor, New York, doing extensive business in Kingston, Upper Canada. John married Jane Carson Turpin in Kingston on January 18, 1817. They had eight children over a twenty-four-year period.

John and Reuben and their families settled in Hamilton, Upper Canada, in 1834. There, the writings of William Lyon Mackenzie appealed to their republican ideals.

Due to John's avid support for political reform and tacit approval of armed rebellion documented in letters to friends, a Tory mob broke into his house, roughed up his wife and hauled him to jail on December 5, 1837, two days before Mackenzie's defeat at Toronto. While Parker was guilty of no more than an unpopular opinion, the government convicted him of treason and

John G. Parker carved this small wooden box, now on display at Fort Henry, in August 1838 after his failed escape. *Photo by the author.*

sentenced him to transport for life in the Van Diemen's Land penal colony. (Colonial authorities also arrested Reuben, thirty-seven, on suspicion and released him on bail six months later.)

Parker, forty-four, waited six months in the Toronto jail crammed into small rooms with political prisoners before being shipped to Fort Henry. Once at the fort, he plotted with John Montgomery to escape. Parker succeeded in breaking out on July 29 but separated from the others. Six miles away, a corporal recaptured him and turned down a $900 bribe to set Parker free.

While in captivity in Toronto and Kingston, Parker partook in a popular prison pastime: the carving of small wooden boxes from chunks of firewood. Using pocketknives, scrap metal and glass shards, they carved, polished and inscribed their creations. Most became gifts for friends and bear the recipient's name. Inscriptions included religious messages, political comments or the names of martyrs, such as Samuel Lount. Historians estimate that Toronto's Patriot inmates made at least one hundred boxes, of which eighty survive in museums and private collections. Parker appears to be the only box carver at Fort Henry.

The memoirs of Charles Durand, one of Parker's cellmates, suggest they created two hundred or more boxes of various types:

> *During the week days the prisoners used to make all kinds of memento boxes of cedar and Canadian maple wood boxes for snuff, for needles, money or rings. On these boxes all kinds of mottoes would be written in indelible ink, and the names of their dearest outside friends, wives, sisters, mothers, and sweethearts, were remembered. The boxes were really very beautiful, with carefully-fitted sliding lids. Hundreds were sent out to friends…*

Parker carved two boxes while in Toronto (one with John Montgomery) and another in Fort Henry following his failed escape. The latter, now on display at the fort, measures four inches by two and five-sixteenths inches by two inches and appears to be made of pine. It has a carefully fitted sliding dovetail lid. The inscription written in ink on one long face reads:

to Mrs. John G. Parker
from her affectionate husband, a state
prisoner in
Fort Henry
1 Aug. 1838
Re-imprisoned and put in shackles six feet long

On the other long face, Parker wrote part of a poem from memory called "The Gracious Dedication" written in 1814 by Elizabeth Sarah Garrington. The two narrow box ends read:

Equal Rights
[and]
Civil and Religious Liberty

Short Hills Prisoners Arrive at Fort Henry

On August 23, authorities shipped the fifteen Short Hills captives from Niagara to the fort in Kingston and berthed them in Montgomery's vacated and repaired casement. Colonel Allan Macdonell, the district sheriff and their principal keeper, made certain that his men closely examined prison casements every day. There would be no more escapes.

Patriot captive David Taylor caught a bad cold in Niagara that worsened in Fort Henry. Linus Miller claimed the fort doctor had visited the sick man but provided no medicine and refused to move him to a hospital. He died on August 27, probably of pneumonia.

Sir George Arthur visited Fort Henry to interview the Short Hills prisoners. According to Miller, the lieutenant governor offered him a pardon:

I have sent for you, to learn whether you are sensible of your error with regard
to the crime of which you have been convicted. I wish you to understand me.

I have become interested in your case, chiefly because I believe you to have been sincere in your conduct; and the lancers, whose lives you saved, have been interceding with me, in your behalf. Take time to consider, before you answer my question. Can you say that you are sorry for what you have done, and promise, if I should grant you a free pardon, to go home and follow your profession, without taking any further part in the rebellion? Unless you will do this I cannot befriend you.

Miller thanked Arthur but said he could not make that promise. Arthur returned to the fort later and repeated the offer. Miller again declined. The idealistic and stubborn Miller may have sung a different tune if he knew the brutal realities that faced him in the Tasmanian penal colony.

11

Hunters Lodge Plans Takeover of Canada

September 1838

S ince its founding in May 1838, the Hunters Lodge had achieved a significant level of political influence and military muscle. It had gathered money ($150,000 or more) and large stores of arms, stolen or purchased.

From September 16 to 22, 160 Hunters held a convention in Cleveland, Ohio, to pick new leaders for pending invasions of Canada that fall, to create a provisional government and to lay the groundwork for their financial arm, the Republican Bank of Canada. (The bank's notes were to bear the faces of Patriot martyrs Samuel Lount, Peter Matthews and James Morreau.)

The big names in the Patriot and Hunter organizations attended, as did ambitious new leaders.

Bill Johnston forsook his island refuge for Cleveland's bustling streets. Donald McLeod joined him, likely seeing Bill for the first time since they burned the *Sir Robert Peel*. Patriot stalwarts Dr. Charles Duncombe and General Henry S. Handy (leader of the western Patriots) attended, as did representatives of Lower Canada's Patriote leader Robert Nelson. No one invited William Lyon Mackenzie, the man who started it all.

The conventioneers elected Abram Daniel Smith, twenty-seven, then the chief justice of the peace in Cleveland, as president. Had the Hunters succeeded in overthrowing Upper Canada and establishing a republican government, President Smith's face would grace Canada's ten-dollar bill today, not that of Prime Minister Macdonald.

The convention reaffirmed Bill Johnston as navy commodore in the St. Lawrence River and Lake Ontario. Gilman Appleby, the captain of the ill-fated *Caroline*, became navy commodore on Lake Erie. Donald McLeod rose to secretary of war.

The delegates elected Connecticut-born Lucius Verus Bierce, thirty-seven, from Akron, Ohio, a brigadier general in the state militia, as the Hunter army's commander in chief.

Spies for both nations at the convention reported the events. Among the spooks was Heley Chamberlain. A Hunter Lodge member, he proved to be Upper Canada's most effective spy.

Following the convention, Hunter leaders in the West and East spoke of simultaneous attacks in November near Windsor and on the St. Lawrence River. Patriote leader Robert Nelson also picked November for his next assault on Lower Canada.

Bernard Bagley

Bernard Bagley, Bill Johnston's lawyer friend from Watertown, became a vice-president of the new Republican Bank of Canada at the convention. Bagley exemplified the type of civic leader who threw support behind the Patriot and Hunter movements, though few prominent Americans immersed themselves in the Patriot cause to his extent.

He was born in Durham, New York, one of a family with six sons and two daughters. He came to Jefferson County in 1812 and settled in Antwerp. He taught school, took road-building contracts and worked as a constable.

In 1815 or 1816, Bagley settled in Pamelia, Jefferson County, and entered the law office of Charles E. Clarke in nearby Watertown as a law student. Bagley was called to the bar in 1826. He quickly became a trial lawyer, locally famous for his instinctive knowledge of human nature. Bagley also impressed people with his voluminous memory and workload. At trials, he never referred to notes or briefs but could recall extensive details as needed.

In 1823 or 1824, he married Zerviah Wright, a young widow and mother. They had two children, Bernard and George.

Bagley contributed greatly to the Patriot War on multiple fronts. Besides his role in the Hunters bank, Bagley corresponded regularly with William Lyon Mackenzie and Bill Johnston. He helped acquit *Peel* pirate William Anderson, and he prepared Mackenzie's defense against Neutrality Act charges.

A letter printed in the *Watertown Herald* on August 19, 1893, suggests he also smuggled arms for the cause. His son George (then a former U.S. congressmen) wrote how, when a youth, he discovered one hundred kegs of gunpowder under hay in the family barn. Later, the kegs disappeared.

The few surviving handwritten documents with Bill Johnston's signature prove he was barely literate, yet all his published letters and proclamations show skill in grammar, spelling, composition and argument. He clearly had onc or more ghost writers. The legal tone of many Johnston texts hints at Bagley's involvement.

12

New York Hunters Prepare for the War's Biggest Raid

October 1838

While Generals Lucius Bierce and Donald McLeod cautiously plotted raids on Upper Canada, an independent Hunter division assembled in northeastern New York in the autumn of 1838. Commanded by John Ward Birge, thirty-one, the army boasted a stunning amount of artillery and modern rifles and thousands of volunteer recruits.

Birge was born in Litchfield, Connecticut. He later settled in Cazenovia, New York, and became a pharmacist, dentist and state militia officer. He married Charlotte James in 1832. In 1838, Birge joined the Hunters Lodge in Salina, near Syracuse, New York, and rose through the ranks to lead all lodges in Onondaga County. At the Hunter convention in Cleveland that September, delegates appointed Birge general of an independent Hunter division in upstate New York. That was a mistake.

New York Hunter leaders wanted to fight and felt held back by the "westerners" in Cleveland. Without any coordination or communication with Bierce and McLeod, Birge organized his own invasion of Upper Canada.

At a Hunters Lodge meeting in late October 1838, Birge, at his bumptious best, promised the assembled men that at least twenty thousand fighters were ready to overrun Upper Canada and set the Canadians free. Further, he assured them that 90 percent of Canadian colonists and 75 percent of Canadian troops would flock to the Hunter banner. He also promised one hundred acres of confiscated farmland to anyone who landed on the Canadian shore in the planned assault. The Hunter ranks lapped it up, without question.

Heustis and other Hunter officers used the comfortable rooms of the Union Hotel in Sackets Harbor as their headquarters.

The building that housed the Union Hotel in Sackets Harbor, New York, in 1838 remains in use today. *Photo by the author.*

Birge attracted a core of respected officers. Martin Woodruff, forty, from Salina, joined Birge as a colonel. Daniel George, twenty-seven, a teacher and senior Hunter from Lyme, Jefferson County, became paymaster. Dorephus Abbey, forty-seven, from Pamelia, a former newspaper publisher, militia officer and Hunter leader, became a colonel. John Kimball, a Hunter recruiter from Dexter, Jefferson County, also became a colonel.

Birge's captains and junior officers were Americans: Christopher Buckley, thirty, a salt manufacturer from Salina; Aaron Dresser, twenty-two, from Alexandria, Jefferson County; Sylvester Lawton, twenty-eight, from Lyme; and John Thomas, twenty-seven, from Madrid, Jefferson County. James Philips, thirty-eight, was the lone Canadian officer. Lyman Leach, forty, from Salina, Onondaga County, a veteran of the Hickory Island, also signed up.

To Captain Daniel Heustis, thirty-two, Birge gave command of the Hunter garrison in Sackets Harbor, New York.

One notable Hunter warrior that Birge did not entice to join him was Bill Johnston. As Hunter admiral and local lodge leader, Johnston was surely privy to Birge's plans. He may have offered advice but avoided aligning himself with the impatient general. Johnston didn't avoid that battle to come; he participated on his own terms.

Nils von Schoultz

Notable among Birge's colonels was Nils Sholtewskii von Schoultz, thirty-one, a man with aristocratic bearing and a colorful past. Von Schoultz was born in Finland, served in a Swedish artillery regiment, fought the Russians in Poland with Polish freedom fighters and served with the French Foreign Legion in Africa. He married in 1834 but abandoned his wife when he moved to the United States in 1836. He became a successful salt manufacturer in Salina.

Stephen Smith Wright, twenty-five, from Denmark, Lewis County, described von Schoultz thus in his memoirs:

Image of Nils Sholtewskii von Schoultz, the leader of the raiders at the Battle of the Windmill.

> *His height was five feet eleven, with firm and graceful limbs, with a well-bred gentleness in his manners, and an eye which blazed in its own liquid light. It was very rarely he smiled, but when he did it was as sunshine through prison bars; with a kind heart and as noble a soul as ever was found in fetters of clay, he was one whose very faults leaned towards virtue's side.*

Intrigued by how closely the conversations on Canadian liberation matched his experiences in Poland, von Schoultz joined the Hunters. He offered his services and five hundred Polish exiles to General Lucius Bierce for the pending invasion of Canada. Bierce thanked him but did not close the deal. Birge convinced the naïve von Schoultz to join him instead.

WILLIAM ESTES

John Birge also aligned himself with William Estes, thirty-four, a businessman and land speculator from Cape Vincent, New York, who arrogated the title of general.

Cape Vincent grave of General William Estes, the man who conceived the Hunter raid on Canada near Prescott. *Photo by the author.*

Born to Benjamin Estes and Phebe Borland in Cape Vincent, New York, the eleventh of twelve children, Estes developed early business and community connections. He became a local Mason lodge leader before the age of thirty and a commissioned officer in the state militia a few years later. He married twice and had five children with his first wife, Helen, and two with his second wife, Betsey.

As Heustis noted in his memoirs, Estes, more than any other, influenced the target of the proposed invasion:

About this time, a plan was maturing in our lodge meetings for another attempt to hoist the patriot standard on the soil of Canada. It was at first understood that the expedition was to start in November, and go by way of Cleveland, where it would be joined by a large force raised in that vicinity. At a meeting of the leaders or officers at Watertown, General Estes proposed that instead of going to Cleveland, we should go down the St. Lawrence and land at Prescott, a small town opposite Ogdensburg. There was considerable difference of opinion as to the best plan, but the majority finally adopted the proposition of General Estes.

The choice of Prescott as a target ranks as one of the worst decisions of the Patriot War in the East.

13

Stage Set for Bloodiest Month of the Patriot War

November 1838

On November 9, 1838, guards at Fort Henry in Kingston told the surviving Short Hills captives to prepare to leave within an hour on the first leg of their trip to the distant penal colony of Van Diemen's Land. Guards bound them so quickly in irons that few had time to write final letters to family, according to Linus Miller.

Benjamin Wait received a last visit from his ever loyal wife, Maria. Sheriff Macdonell allowed them minutes alone in a separate room.

The prisoners marched to Navy Bay at the fort's base and boarded the *Cobourg*, a civilian steamer leased by the Royal Navy. With them were Leonard Watson and John G. Parker, two men who had failed to escape with Montgomery, and six Patriots condemned for various raids in the rebellion's early days.

As they cruised among the Thousand Islands, Miller related that William Reynolds recounted his days serving in the islands with Bill Johnston. Reynolds remarked how he wished Johnston would attack them like he did the *Sir Robert Peel*.

On November 10, they transferred ships in Prescott and continued. Shortly, they passed a stately stone windmill. They had no way of predicting the historic role that windmill was soon to play.

Steaming along the river in Lower Canada, depredation and devastation lay over the countryside. Days earlier, Robert Nelson's Patriotes had swept in from Vermont. The British quickly defeated them and commenced a series of reprisals that continued for weeks. Benjamin Wait recalled seeing farmhouses, barns and the entire village of Beauharnois completely in ruins due to retaliatory fires.

Miller and his companions changed ships in Montreal and sailed on to Quebec City. Confined on board a lumber ship, they set sail on November 22. Wait wrote that while in transit to England, prisoners plotted to overthrow the crew. However, fellow rebel Jacob Beemer informed the captain in the hope of a reprieve for himself. With all the traitor accusations against Beemer, it is surprising that none of his comrades slit his throat.

On December 16, 1838, they arrived at Portsmouth, England, where the English split them into two groups. One went to the infamous Newgate Prison, a cesspool of human incarceration. Ten others languished for months on a prison hulk moored in Portsmouth Harbor, shivering in the ship's unheated bowels.

Birge Puts War in Motion

In early November 1838, Hunter general John Ward Birge ordered his troops to assemble for war at various towns along eastern Lake Ontario and the Thousand Islands. He timed it to coincide with a state election so that crowds of strangers on the move would not arouse suspicions.

Under Birge's plan, unarmed men were to board the passenger steamer *United States* in Oswego on November 8. Small bands of Hunters were to embark at each town where the steamer stopped on its scheduled route to Ogdensburg.

With his orders given, General Birge took a coach ahead of the steamer to organize more men in Ogdensburg, the American town directly across the river from the attack target: Prescott, Upper Canada.

The first crack in Birge's tidy plan came when the steamer's boilers malfunctioned. The *United States* could not leave on schedule, with a costly result, as noted by Captain Heustis:

> *It had originally been agreed that our men should assemble at Sackets Harbor, on the 5th of November, and take passage on board the steamer* United States, *Captain Van Cleve, a regular packet boat, running between Oswego and Ogdensburg. The arrangements not being completed, we did not embark until the 11th. Some five or six hundred men arrived at Sackets Harbor on the 5th, and after remaining there several days, returned to their homes. Thus much we lost by bad management at the outset.*

Eastern Lake Ontario map by John Melish, 1815, showing towns the steamer *United States* visited en route to the windmill battle. *David Rumsey Map Collection.*

A long list of books written by historians—well known and little known alike—since the mid-nineteenth century say that Bill Johnston captained one of the two schooners. That is fiction. No account by participants (Heustis, Gates and Wright) or observers (Lieutenant Colonel Bonnycastle) places Johnston on either schooner. (See bibliography for details.)

On November 10, two hired schooners, the *Charlotte of Oswego* (Captain William Sprague) and *Charlotte of Toronto* (Captain Quick) set sail from Oswego, New York. Carrying troops commanded by Colonel Nils von Schoultz, the ships headed toward the Thousand Islands. Onboard were six cannons ranging from a puny three-pounder to a lethal eighteen-pounder. Crates of modern rifles, including the recently invented multiple-round rifles; ammunition; food; medical supplies; and other kit of war crammed the holds.

Hunter admiral Bill Johnston took no part in Birge's conspiracy but knew the details. He rowed to Ogdensburg ahead of the attack on Prescott. The reason, as he cryptically explained to friends and family, was "that way I can stay out of the way of all parties."

Spies Report Hunter Activity

By late 1838, his usefulness over, the British ended Chamberlain's employment. Constables arrested him for vagrancy on January 17, 1839, at Henderson near Sackets Harbor.

Spies in upstate New York within the Hunter ranks sent regular reports to military authorities in Canada. On November 10, Heley Chamberlain, a Hunter spying for the British, told Captain Williams Sandom that a Hunter force was bound for Prescott. Sandom, fifty-three, the naval commander on Lake Ontario and a career veteran of sixty naval engagements, sounded the alarm and ordered armed steamers to patrol the lake and the St. Lawrence River.

HUNTER FIGHTERS HIJACK STEAMER

Delayed for three days by boiler repairs, the *United States* readied to disembark on the morning of Sunday, November 11, 1838.

As Captain James Van Cleve, thirty, prepared to cast off, a long column of passengers in civilian clothes—mostly young men with no baggage—boarded. Senior Hunter officers Martin Woodruff, Dorephus Abbey and Daniel George mingled with the new passengers.

Van Cleve later insisted that he and his officers knew the passengers were bent on making trouble, and he did not want to disembark. One of the ship's owners onboard, Hiram Denio, overruled him.

At midday, the *United States* stopped in Sackets Harbor. Captain Daniel Heustis and twenty-nine men waited to board—all that remained of five hundred once-eager Hunter recruits.

In his memoirs, Heustis recalled his conversation at Sackets Harbor when Colonel Woodruff came down the gangplank to confer:

> *"Good day, Colonel."*
> *"Good day to you, Captain. How many men have you?"*

Sketch of the side-wheeler *United States* by William James Thomson, 1893. The steamer was typical of river and lake steamers at the time.

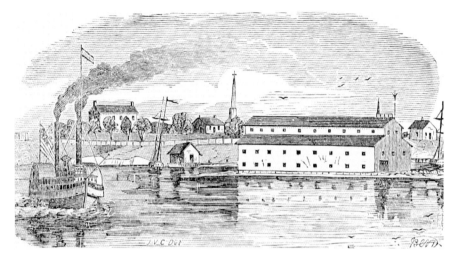

Sketch of Sackets Harbor, New York, by Captain James Van Cleve, circa 1852, included in a travelers' handbook from the St. Lawrence Steamboat Company.

"Besides myself, I have twenty-nine. Have you the five hundred Polanders from New York?"

"Only six have come."

"What is your strength altogether, Colonel?"

"Only one hundred and sixty."

"So few! Our scheme will fail, I fear. We shall be defeated."

"I am aware of it," Woodruff said. "But I can't back out now and neither can you. I'd prefer to be shot. We must go and do our best."

"I will go," Heustis conceded. "I would rather die than be branded a coward. Whatever might be the issue, we ought to meet it as men fighting in a good cause."

The *United States* sailed to Cape Vincent, New York, where more Hunters boarded.

Farther east, at Millens Bay, the two Hunter schooners lay at anchor. Daniel George, pretending to be a businessman needing to sail his ships to Ogdensburg in unfavorable winds, paid Captain Van Cleve $100 to tow the schooners. In proper business fashion, the captain gave George receipts, which he pocketed. With a schooner lashed on each side, the *United States* continued downstream.

When the steamer pulled away from the Clayton wharf an hour later, the schooners' true purpose became apparent. On the *Charlotte of Toronto*,

Cape Vincent, New York, by Captain James Van Cleve.

Ogdensburg, New York, by Captain James Van Cleve. Both sketches, circa 1852, were included in a travelers' handbook from the St. Lawrence Steamboat Company.

von Schoultz emerged into the daylight with a scabbard visible beneath his long cloak. Hundreds of men flooded from the holds of both schooners. They pried open the crates lashed to the decks and armed themselves with rifles. The Hunter army sailing to Prescott now numbered four hundred, and Captain Van Cleve was no longer in control of his ship.

Von Schoultz conferred with the Hunter officers. General Birge had ordered the fleet to stop at Ogdensburg to pick up more recruits. Von Schoultz wanted to sail straight to Prescott, believing that men might desert at Ogdensburg. All officers agreed.

That evening, as the *United States* approached Morristown, New York, officers ordered all Hunters to board the schooners. Half refused. Von Schoultz put Colonel Dorephus Abbey in charge of the deserters on the steamer, hoping he'd change their minds. The schooners cut their bonds and, with a diminished force, sailed into the dark night.

At Morristown, Captain Van Cleve informed authorities of his ship's hijacking and then continued to Ogdensburg, reaching the city at 3:00 a.m. on November 12. Minutes earlier, the passengers heard a rapid series of musket shots echoing from the Canadian shore.

Benjamin Lett Begins His Personal War

Throughout the Patriot War, the majority of Patriot and Hunter raiders followed rules of engagement on par with the British. That is, they generally behaved as soldiers not murderers. While the colonial government called them pirates and brigands, the rebels were no more prone to abuses on the battlefield than the Upper Canadians. There was one notable exception, however: Benjamin Lett.

Lett, twenty-five, was born in County Kilkenny, Ireland, to Samuel Lett and Elizabeth Warren. They immigrated to Lower Canada in 1819 and settled northwest of Montreal.

In September 1824, Samuel died from a fall, leaving his widow and seven young children to fend for themselves. In 1833, Elizabeth relocated her children (consisting of Benjamin, Robert, Thomas, Elizabeth, Anne, Maria and Sarah) to a farm in Upper Canada by Lake Ontario, east of Toronto.

Benjamin Lett took up the reform banner in the 1830s but did not start out as a rebel. He was radicalized by the brutality of loyalist gangs in Upper Canada in the days following Mackenzie's uprising. Usually referred to as

Tory mobs or Orangemen, they terrorized reform sympathizers while the colonial government ignored their thuggery. Lett, himself an Orangeman, refused to join a marauding mob and was in turn set upon. Legend has it—and it may be apocryphal—that Lett's hatred for the Canadian establishment solidified into rage when loyalists shot one of his brothers and sexually abused a sister.

Sources described Lett as five feet, eleven inches tall, and slim with sandy hair and whiskers. He had a ruddy and freckled face, light skin, penetrating light blue eyes and large and muscular hands with long fingers.

Lett joined Mackenzie on Navy Island as a private and was one of the few men wounded there. Published accounts state that he wore four pistols and a Bowie knife hidden under his coat once he turned rebel.

After Lett departed Navy Island in January 1838, he fought in two battles with the western Patriots. Later, it seems he fell in league with a small band of freelance rebels unsanctioned by the Patriot or Hunter leadership.

Lett harbored a grudge concerning the *Caroline*, and he made it his personal business to avenge that act. Late on November 15, 1838, while all eyes watched the siege of Hunters near Prescott, Upper Canada, Lett and two accomplices crossed the Niagara River by boat from Navy Island. At dawn, they visited the home of Captain Edgeworth Ussher. He had piloted Captain Andrew Drew's fleet of boats during the attack on the *Caroline*.

Ussher awoke and sleepily answered a knock on the door. Seeing armed men, he slammed it shut. Lett fired his pistol through the sidelight, killing his victim instantly with a ball in the heart.

Sir George Arthur posted a reward of £500 for Lett and demanded that the American government capture and return the murderer. The comeback from New York secretary of state John C. Spencer, fifty, was priceless. He agreed to give Lett up if Arthur handed over Colonel Allan MacNab and Captain Andrew Drew for the murder of Amos Durfee.

By that point, the queen had knighted Colonel MacNab for the *Caroline* raid that killed Durfee—a fact Spencer surely knew.

Arthur soon had more reasons to post rewards for Benjamin Lett.

14

Ideals and Armies Clash at the Windmill

November 1838

When the two Hunter schooners cut loose from the steamer, they sailed downstream under a sliver of moon. Guided by the shoreline's loom, the helmsmen sought the lamplights of Prescott, Upper Canada.

Colonel von Schoultz pulled his senior officers together and outlined his plan. He intended to land at the Prescott Harbor and organize the men into three groups. His principal objective was to capture Fort Wellington to the east of town. He told his men he expected little resistance. General John Ward Birge had assured him that Canadians would flock to the Hunters as liberators.

Von Schoultz was duped. General Birge and his advisors chose the most loyal county in Upper Canada to attack, the center of the United Empire Loyalist settlements. Also, by then, every Upper Canada colonist knew of Birge's plan to confiscate Canadian land to reward American raiders. Instead of a friendly welcome, the Hunters faced determined and vengeful defenders.

Favorable winds blew the schooners close to Prescott. Upstream from town, the schooner crews dropped the sails and lashed the vessels together. They drifted through the predawn mist toward Prescott. As they came upon the wharf, John Cronkhite, twenty-nine, a blacksmith from Alexandria, Oswego County, jumped onto the dock and attempted to make fast the ships. He reboarded just as the rope broke.

Guards in Prescott spotted the suspicious ships and fired their muskets. A surprise assault now futile, von Schoultz ordered the ships to raise sail and cross the river to Ogdensburg.

An 1836 map of Ogdensburg, New York, shows the town as it existed in 1838 when the Hunters briefly controlled its waterfront.

As the sun rose that cold morning of November 12, 1838, curious Ogdensburg residents and Hunter fighters crowding the waterfront witnessed the embarrassing result of the Hunters' aborted raid. The two hired schooner captains, unfamiliar with the local waters, had run both ships onto a mud shoal in American waters.

BILL JOHNSTON HELPS WINDMILL RAIDERS

Bill Johnston rowed to the stranded vessels and took charge as the Hunter navy's admiral. He had men offload munitions from the *Charlotte of Toronto* onto a scow. The lightened schooner refloated and slipped into deeper water.

As Johnston worked his magic, General Birge visited the schooner in a hired rowboat. Captain Daniel Heustis later described his actions:

> *On the morning of the 12th, while the schooners were in the situation just described, he came along side of us in a small boat, but did not come on board. I asked him what was to be done. He said we must go ashore, and*

The flag that flew over the windmill during the Hunter occupation looked much like this. After the trials, the colony shipped the flag to England, where it was lost in a fire.

get the cannon ashore as quick as possible. He then pulled for Ogdensburg, and I have never seen the coward since.

Colonel Nils von Schoultz ordered the free schooner to cross the river to a point one mile downstream from Prescott. Johnston followed in the scow with ammunition and two small cannons he had liberated from Ogdensburg arsenals. Because of shallow water, the ship anchored a distance from shore. A flotilla of small boats carried the Hunter fighters to the rocky beach.

Von Schoultz, Captain Daniel Heustis and ten men landed first. They immediately took possession of a six-story windmill, perched five yards from the steep river bank. On its peak, they raised the Onondaga Hunters' flag. Made, as Heustis said, "by the patriotic ladies of Onondaga County," it bore an eagle and two stars.

Just beyond the former wind-powered flour mill sat the hamlet of Newport (now called Wexford), a cluster of eleven stone buildings and a wooden barn. Von Schoultz displayed sound military sense in choosing Newport as the place to make a stand. The stone structures would keep his men safe from musket fire and low-caliber artillery. The windmill, perched high beside the river on a steep bank and boasting round, four-foot-thick walls, offered the

The indestructible old windmill, now an out-of-service lighthouse, still dominates the shoreline above steep cliffs. *Photo by the author.*

same military advantage as a Mortello tower—a commanding structure resistant to cannonballs.

As more men disembarked, the Hunters took over the barn and all unoccupied buildings (most residents fled). They stored powder and ammunition in the windmill. Von Schoultz commandeered the three-story tavern for his headquarters. Gunners set up a battery behind a makeshift stone wall.

Snipers took positions in windows. From their high vantage points, they had a clear view of a naval encounter unfolding in the river.

NAVAL BATTLE BEGINS

While Colonel Nils von Schoultz unloaded raiders and munitions from the *Charlotte of Toronto* at the windmill midmorning on November 12, 1838, the second and larger Hunter schooner remained stuck in the mud. It held the bulk of their supplies, including all their large field pieces.

General John Birge, in his only meaningful battle involvement, attempted to free the grounded ship. He marched from his headquarters at the Ogdensburg customhouse at the head of one hundred armed Hunters.

The customhouse used briefly as General John Ward Birge's headquarters exists today on the Ogdensburg waterfront. *Photo by the author.*

They hijacked the *United States* for the second time in as many days. With the steamer's crew operating the equipment, the side-wheeler set out.

The mud shoal prevented the *United States* from getting close to the stranded schooner, and no rope on board was found to be long enough. Birge ordered the ship to Ogdensburg for more rope.

William Newton Fowell, thirty-five, an ambitious Royal Navy lieutenant, observed Birge's first attempt. Fowell commanded the *Experiment*, a small (150-ton) single-engine steamer armed with an eighteen-pound carronade (a short naval cannon) and a three-pound swivel gun.

On Birge's second attempt to tow the schooner, the *United States* crossed into Canadian waters. Fowell pounced. In the wheelhouse with Birge were Oliver Pierce, twenty-nine, and Solomon Foster (approximately eighteen). None of them had any business being in a naval battle.

Pierce was a Hunter officer (rank unknown) with no military experience. He worked as a teacher and lecturer, specializing in grammar. He dabbled in inventions and is said to have designed a rudimentary submarine. A proponent of temperance and abolition, he seemed drawn to noble causes.

Foster was a river rat, a young man who lived by the St. Lawrence all his life and became a pilot and helmsman at an early age. He had no Hunter allegiance. Why he stayed on the steamer is unknown. Maybe it was the thrill of adventure. Maybe the sight of his uncle, Henry Shew, twenty-nine, among the Hunter ranks gave the affair legitimacy.

At full speed, the *Experiment* bore down on the larger ship. Hunters on board the *United States* peppered Fowell's ship with rifle fire. The small steamer ignored the whizzing bullets and let loose a round from both guns. The *Experiment*'s gunners reloaded and fired another round as they passed by.

Accounts of the accuracy of Fowell's gunners vary. Some sources, mostly Canadian, say all rounds hit the big ship but did no serious damage. Other sources, mostly American, say the shots missed. Whatever the truth, the encounter left the *United States* unscathed.

Seconds after the boom of Fowell's guns swept the river, Birge had a sudden attack of "seasickness" and retired to a stateroom, leaving Pierce in command. A man for all occasions, Pierce rose to the challenge and ordered the steamer downriver. He placed it and its sharpshooter occupants between the *Experiment* and the *Charlotte of Toronto* as it disembarked seventy Hunter raiders. With the men ashore, the schooner and steamer returned to the American shore.

In the meantime, Hunters in Ogdensburg commandeered the *Paul Pry*, a fifty-ton, shallow-draft steam ferry, and successfully towed the *Charlotte of Oswego* off the mud. Fowell's *Experiment* hurled multiple rounds of cannonballs and grapeshot at both the little ferry and the schooner from inside Canadian waters.

To Fowell's surprise, the schooner fought back. A field gun stored on deck discharged a round at the *Experiment*. According to Heustis, Isaac Tiffany loaded and aimed the piece, but Orrin W. Smith, twenty-eight, a farmer from Orleans in Jefferson County, fired it. (That was Tiffany's only military contribution. He never crossed to the windmill.)

Some sources, mostly Canadian, say the shot missed. Other sources, mostly American, say the shot swept through the *Experiment* killing and wounding crewmen. Whatever the truth, the *Experiment* retreated. Both American ships returned to Ogdensburg safely, though the schooner's sails had been shredded by the grapeshot.

In the early afternoon, Pierce guided the *United States* back to the Canadian side with 110 Hunters who wanted to join the fight. Bill Johnston greeted the returning steamer and helped unload the men using his own boat. The *Experiment* steamed in circles nearby, keeping well back of three Hunter cannons set up by the windmill. Johnston, frustrated by Fowell's persistence, was heard to exclaim that he had half a mind to board "that damned little boat."

As Pierce returned the big steamer to Ogdensburg, Fowell came out to challenge him again. Pierce, a brave man but not necessarily a practical one, ordered Foster to set a course to ram the *Experiment* to end its meddling. Young Foster, clearly having the most exciting day of his life, did as asked.

The ships headed for a collision at a combined speed of eighteen knots. The 450-ton *United States*, its twin smokestacks exuding plumes of black exhaust, had the advantage over the 150-ton, single-engine *Experiment*. The impact would clearly sink the smaller steamer and might scuttle both.

Pierce's bravery was no match for Fowell's tactical experience. On his orders, his helmsman swerved seconds before contact, and the gunners fired at close range. The eighteen-pounder damaged the starboard paddle-wheel on the *United States*. The small ball passed through its pilothouse, removing half of young Foster's head. The underdog *Experiment* won the day.

The big steamer limped to Ogdensburg. Pierce, Birge and other Hunters disappeared into the crowds.

THE TRAPDOOR CLOSES

Troops under U.S. colonel William Jenkins Worth, forty-four, arrived to enforce the Neutrality Act. He impounded the two Hunter schooners and the *Paul Pry*, effectively cutting off the Hunters' supply route to the windmill. The bulk of Hunter troops, artillery and supplies von Schoultz needed sat inexorably on the wrong side of the river. In addition, the *United States'* crew partly dismantled an engine to prevent further hijackings.

Throughout the night, rowboats made the nine-thousand-foot round trip between the two shores, carrying men in both directions—fighters going north and deserters going south. Colonel John Kimball, aide to Colonel von Schoultz, was the highest-ranking deserter.

Men came to gawk or talk. One was General William Estes. He chatted with von Schoultz, assuring him that more men would arrive, and then boated across to safety.

Witnesses recalled Bill Johnston tirelessly urging Hunters crowding the Ogdensburg port that night to cross to their comrades. Few did. Johnston rowed across at least twice with small groups of men. One recruit was Orrin Smith, who had fired the cannon at the *Experiment* that day. Johnston last visited von Schoultz near midnight. He said Ogdensburg held five hundred Hunters, and he promised to do his best to bring them over.

But Admiral Johnston had no means to keep that promise. Worth had impounded every ship. And now an American steamer, the *Telegraph*, patrolled in mid-river to prevent any further crossings. Its captain was Johnston's old ally from the War of 1812, William Vaughan.

Together, ships from both nations had isolated the Hunter raiders, cutting off supplies and reinforcements. Captain Heustis summed up the first night:

> *During that night, in which no eye slept, we could but realize that our situation was one of extreme peril. In regard to the number expected to join us, we had been woefully disappointed, and of those who had started with us, a large majority had ignobly deserted. Our leaders had also proved traitors and cowards. We had lost much of our ammunition. Our position was exposed to attack, both by land and water, by a force vastly larger than we could muster. Amid all these unfavorable circumstances, foreboding almost certain defeat, there was no repining, no wavering, no flinching from the contest, on the part of the resolute and heroic band of young men at Windmill Point. A braver company never shouldered muskets.*

WINDMILL BATTLE, DAY ONE

The Hunter raiders trapped on a wedge of Upper Canada woke in the cool, bright dawn of Tuesday, November 13, 1838, to see three armed English steamers moving into firing position on the misty St. Lawrence River.

The *Experiment* (150 tons), the *Cobourg* (500 tons) and the *Queen Victory* (200 tons) carried between them seven eighteen-pound carronades and one twelve-pound cannon. At 8:00 a.m., the ships began bombarding the Hunters' fortified hamlet.

Because of the carronades' limited range and power, their projectiles often plowed into the limestone cliffs below the windmill. Those balls that hit the mill or the stone houses in Newport usually bounced off. The Hunter battery returned fire. Their shots fell short but served to keep the enemy ships from coming closer.

That morning, a force of five hundred Canadian militia (farmers, shopkeepers and laborers) in civilian clothes and one hundred professional soldiers in red infantry or blue navy uniforms gathered at Fort Wellington,

This twenty-four-pound carronade at Fort Henry is similar to the eighteen-pounders used on steamers during the Battle of the Windmill. *Photo by the author.*

Painting of a militia encampment beside Fort Wellington near Prescott in 1867 in a scene similar to the events of November 13, 1838.

between Prescott and the windmill. They formed into companies and marched to Newport, surrounding it at 9:00 a.m. The Canadian force had superior numbers and was better prepared—military training being a legal requirement for Upper Canada men.

Captain Daniel Heustis wrote that 182 Hunters fought the first day, mostly untrained teens and young men from farms and villages.

Though fewer in numbers, the Hunters had modern rifles that could shoot farther and more accurately than the militia's muskets. The American farm boys were also crack shots, veterans of turkey shoots and other marksmen contests. (Field reports noted that a high number of British and Canadian casualties had head wounds—a sign of the Hunter sharpshooters' confidence and marksmanship.)

The St. Lawrence River narrows between Prescott and Ogdensburg. Fort Wellington is clearly visible from the American side even today. The hundreds of Ogdensburg residents lining the riverbank watched the drama unfold as ships bombarded the Hunters and regiments of soldiers marched from the fort.

Von Schoultz had two choices. The smart choice was surrender. The loyalist

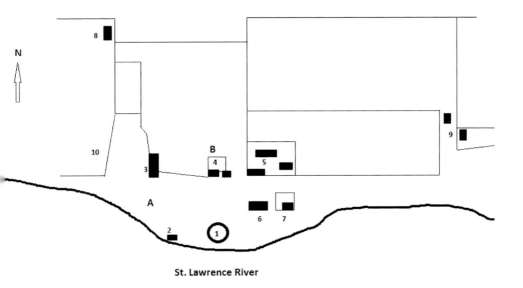

St. Lawrence River

Newport based on a map by Lieutenant Parker: 1) windmill; 2) hut; 3) carriage barn; 4), 5), 7) and 9) houses; 6) tavern; 8) wooden barn; and 10) butternut grove. Thin lines are fences. A) Lieutenant Johnson killed. B) Lieutenant Parker wounded.

army had the rebels clearly outnumbered, surrounded and cut off. But perhaps because he believed the Hunter generals' promise of five hundred more fighters, he chose to fight. He ordered the bulk of his men to exit the buildings and take up positions behind wood and stone fences on the village perimeter.

The Canadian-British force began its lethal march toward central Newport from the north. On both sides, few men had faced a real enemy—this was their first battle. Both sides traded volleys of lead as soon as they got within range.

The Second Grenville militia and Glengarry Highlanders under Colonel Richard Duncan Fraser took the brunt of Hunter fire in that initial encounter. Fraser, fifty-four, was a bombastic and bad-tempered man but a competent officer. A scion of loyalists who had left for Canada after American independence, he served in

One militia squad arrived commanded by Colonel John Crysler, sixty-eight. Born in colonial America, he'd been a drummer boy for a British regiment during the American Revolution and immigrated to Upper Canada with his family after independence. In 1813, he fought for the British at the battle named after his farm.

Fraser's regiment included Privates Alan and Lewis Macintosh. It was on their family farm, twenty miles east, that their father, John, cultivated the crispy red apple variety that still bears the family name.

the artillery during the War of 1812 and as a local militia officer. His temper was legendary, and he had faced assault charges on numerous occasions.

Fraser took the raid personally for two reasons: the Hunters had dared to attack his county, and he knew Bill Johnston was somehow involved. Fraser had been a passenger on the ill-fated *Sir Robert Peel* whom Johnston's bandits had roughed up and robbed six months earlier.

Fraser ordered his men to fix bayonets and charge. The Hunters fired a last round, balked and ran as a wall of resolute, angry and howling men charged through the gunpowder smoke. The Hunters, untrained in close combat, faced men who had drilled for hours on bayonet use. Militiamen skewered slow-running Hunters with lethal seventeen-inch, three-sided blades.

The Hunters retreated into the fortified stone buildings. Snipers firing through windows and doors stopped Fraser's advance.

Colonel Fraser's force included sixty-five men led by First Lieutenant Charles Allan Parker of the Royal Marines. Parker's memoirs provide the only published firsthand account of the Battle of the Windmill from the British perspective.

Lieutenant Parker wrote that he and his men faced withering rifle fire from snipers in the stone buildings. He took a ball in the arm that cut to the bone. Another bullet passed through his hair on the side of his head. He speculated that the Hunters targeted him because he was an officer: "I felt at this time that I was being marked, my dress distinguishing me: the three men nearest to me were struck about the same moment."

After twelve to fourteen minutes pinned down, cannonballs from the steamers in the river landed close to Parker's men, and he ordered a retreat. He wrote that he was glad such circumstances gave him a pretext to fall back. Of his men, five died and twenty-two had wounds.

The steamers kept up a barrage throughout the battle. William Gates, twenty-four, a laborer from Lyme, Jefferson County, recalled being inside the windmill when a cannonball screamed in through a window. It smacked the inside wall with an ear-piercing boom, raising a cloud of old flour dust. Instead of bouncing to the floor where men huddled, it rolled in circles around the windmill's round interior, like a bug swirling down a drain, and settled on the floor, injuring no one. Heat from the eighteen-pound iron ball helped warm the frigid room.

Meanwhile, a second Canadian force commanded by Lieutenant Colonel Olge Gowan, thirty-five, approached Newport from the west through a butternut grove. From behind a stone wall, the Hunters let loose a devastating volley. Once more, the attackers fixed bayonets and charged. Again, the Hunter ranks broke and ran. Snipers in the stone buildings covered their retreating comrades and stopped Gowan's advance.

Nelson Truax, twenty, a saddler from Antwerp, Jefferson County, fought for the Hunters in the grove that day. A musket ball hit his leg, and he fell. As a militiaman readied to bayonet him, a

Portrait of Lieutenant Charles Parker between 1841 and 1847, after his service in Upper Canada.

British regular shoved the man aside and took Truax prisoner, saving his life. That is one of many cases in which calm, professional British soldiers prevented summary executions of Hunters by the angry and hotheaded Canadian militia.

Amidst the noise and confusion, Lieutenant William Johnson, thirty-nine, led a group of men to capture a Hunter cannon. (Heustis wrote that the ordnance was left unattended as a decoy.) In doing so, Johnson and his men walked into a fierce Hunter crossfire from a group of buildings.

Lieutenant Parker chronicled the lieutenant's demise. Johnson gathered his men behind the shelter of a shed and then led a charge over a wall. According to Parker, no sooner had Johnson passed the building than "a shower of bullets" poured on him from nine windows. Hit five times, he died immediately.

Following a brief pause at 10:30 a.m. to regroup, the Canadians charged again. Lieutenant Colonel Plomer Young, forty-one, the local militia commander, and Colonel Fraser entered Newport from the east. Heustis wrote that the Canadian force charged and then feigned a retreat. A band of Hunters eagerly followed and were outflanked and snared in a trap. The enemy captured thirty men and sent dozens of Hunters running for the windmill in a hail of musket balls.

Captain James Philips, thirty-eight, the only Canadian officer in von Schoultz's army, was hit twice and dropped dead. William Gates rose from behind a wall to shoot and found himself alone between his fleeing fellows and Fraser's charging soldiers. He fired the weapon, dropped it and sprinted to the windmill with musket balls whizzing past him.

Despite the setback, the Hunters held that flank.

Shortly after 11:00 a.m., Lieutenant Colonel Young halted the attack. He lacked enough men to overpower the Hunters, and the fleet did not have the fire power to breach the windmill and stone buildings. At 3:00 p.m., Young stationed a cordon of soldiers around Newport and led the bulk of his troops and the Hunter captives to Prescott. The naval bombardment ceased.

In the eerie quiet, the Hunters celebrated their Pyrrhic victory. They had no food and no medical supplies for the wounded. Trapped, they knew the Canadians would return with more men and bigger cannons.

Historic accounts suggest that all Canadian and British casualties at the windmill occurred the first day. The Hunters had approximately eight dead and fourteen wounded (two died that night), plus thirty-two men taken prisoner. Heustis found six bullet tears in his clothing but miraculously avoided the casualty list.

WHO SHOT THE TAYLOR FAMILY?

Early in the fighting on the first day, the lone family remaining in Newport attempted to flee. Three men who wrote eyewitness accounts—Daniel Heustis, Stephen Wright and Lieutenant Charles Parker—gave differing details, though they all agree that a woman, Mrs. Benden Taylor, died that day.

Daniel Heustis wrote that, upon the approach of the Canadian troops, a woman and her teenage daughter attempted to flee from their home to safety but were cut down: "When the fiendish soldiers came within shooting distance of these unprotected females, they fired upon them, killing the mother and badly wounding the daughter in the jaw."

Stephen Wright tells the same story, except he says the woman was carrying a child who died in her arms.

Lieutenant Charles Parker said he observed two women (a pregnant matron and a teenager), a man with a child in his arms and a boy coming toward the Canadian lines. He ordered his enlisted men to cease fire, which they obeyed, while the militia continued shooting. He then ordered them to stop, which they did. Parker discovered that the older women had a mortal wound in her abdomen, and the child was killed in her arms by the same bullet. Parker makes no mention of the fate of the teenage girl, the boy or the man. He also has the child initially in the arms of the man but then killed in the arms of the matron.

In his 1938 account of the battle published in the *Watertown Daily Times*, historian John Northman gave the following details based on a newspaper report of an interview with the fleeing man in the story (presumably Benden Taylor):

> *As the Canadians drew close to one of the houses, a man emerged with a three-year-old child in his arms, followed by his wife, daughter and a little boy. Excited militiamen fired at them. The mother fell mortally wounded and died in two hours. The daughter was shot in the jaw and disfigured for life. Taylor was spared a similar fate when a man in the militia ranks recognized him and knocked aside a musket aimed his way.*

Northman's account does not mention the child's death.

Heustis and Wright both composed their memoirs years after the tragedy. Lieutenant Charles Parker presumably updated his journal within days. Lieutenant Parker's account bears up well, especially when compared to Northman's research.

Based on the various accounts, we know for sure that Mrs. Benden Taylor died, and her teenage daughter Eliza took a musket ball in her jaw. Strong evidence suggests that a child died in its mother's arms and that Mr. Taylor and the boy survived.

But who shot the Taylor family? Heustis and Wright blame the Canadians. Lieutenant Parker implicates the militia and never blamed the Hunters. Had he a shred of evidence that the Hunters (to whom he always referred as brigands and pirates) fired the fatal shots, he would have stated it.

Six months later, Eliza Taylor visited Daniel Heustis during his confinement in Fort Henry. Her visit clearly shows that she did not view Heustis and the Hunters as complicit in her mother's death.

The weight of evidence points to a group of nervous Canadian reservists overreacting in the fear, smoke and thunder of their first battle.

Von Schoultz Tries to Contact Birge

Winter arrived that afternoon. Snow soon shrouded the unclaimed bodies in the battlefield's no-man's land. As night approached, Colonel Nils von Schoultz made two attempts to deliver a message to General John Ward Birge on the American side.

In the short November day's fading light, the Hunters found a leaky old boat (but no oars) on the beach. Four Americans set off to cross the river with a message for Birge requesting food and medical supplies. William Gates, who was in the boat, named Daniel George, Charles Smith and Aaron Dresser as his companions.

The men took advantage of a gap in the gunboat patrols and stroked toward the invisible river border as fast as they could with crude paddles made of boards. The steamer *Cobourg* emerged from the dusk. Its big guns fired. Geysers erupted near the boat as cannonballs plunged into the water. The fleeing men paddled faster. The steamer's cannon boomed again. Its load of grapeshot caused simultaneous splashes near the boat. Gates's crew pressed on. Witnesses that evening swore that the fleeing Hunters had crossed into American waters by that point.

The *Cobourg*, under Captain Williams Sandom, ignored the border and came within musket range. English marines fired on the boat's occupants. Musket balls whizzed past their heads. As the big steamer closed in, the Hunters surrendered. Marines hauled them aboard and frisked each man. In Daniel George's pockets, they found receipts from Captain Van Cleve for towing the two rebel schooners on November 11. William Gates got lippy and was knocked unconscious.

After dark, a young man named Tom Meredith, a Hunter spy in Prescott who had joined the raiders the previous evening, volunteered to cross the river. He built a narrow raft from fence rails and an old board and set out to cross 1,500 yards of near-freezing water in the cold, snow and darkness. Despite the odds of success, he made it to Ogdensburg and sought out Birge.

Meredith may have had a companion. Maria Knapp, who at age 12 lived in Prescott in 1838, recalled details of the battle eighty-five years later. (She died in 1927 at 101.) She said:

> *There were two spies who lived in Prescott, Tom Meredith and a man named Dinsdale. They acted as guides to the invaders but when the fighting got hot and it looked as though the rebels were beaten, they made a raft out of some fence rails and paddled across the river, probably going to*

Ogdensburg. That was the last ever seen of them in Prescott, although both were property owners there.

Two hours after midnight, Meredith awoke the sleeping general in an Ogdensburg hotel. Meredith demanded that Birge do something. In response, Birge composed a letter to Bill Johnston dated November 14, 1838:

Dear Johnston,
The fate of the men on the other side of the river is in your hands. Nothing is expected of the British above Prescott; and if you can rally your men and go to Jones's Mills and kindle some fires, you will save the men and save Canada. Start fires also at Gananoque and the British will think Kingston is being attacked. Do, for God's sake, rally your men and start immediately.
J. Ward Birge

With his letter, Birge created a publicly credible but militarily impossible solution to the tragedy unfolding at Newport. Simultaneously, he set up Johnston to become a partial scapegoat for the Hunter defeat at Newport.

Meredith failed to locate Johnston on the streets of Ogdensburg. Bill later said he spent two days and nights scanning the battle from a roof near the harbor.

This engraving of an 1840 print by William Henry Bartlett shows Prescott and Fort Wellington from Ogdensburg, New York, much as it looked in 1838.

The dwindling force of Hunters huddled around fires fed by a meager supply of firewood—bits of roofs torn off by cannonballs. Stephen Wright wrote in his memoirs:

The night was lonely—perhaps the loneliest that it ever will be my lot to experience: the wind whistled shrilly through the arms of the old mill, blending with the groans of the stricken and the dying, who lay shelterless in the night's wild storm.

Heustis wrote that they had only straw pallets for beds and no blankets for the wounded. Still, he retained his sense of purpose:

We felt conscious of having struck a blow in the cause of freedom, which, if not completely successful, would at least save us from the disgraceful reputation of being afraid of the British lion. With all the dark prospect before us, we had no anxiety to exchange situations with the cowards who had deserted before they got within sight of the enemy, and who had that day stood upon the opposite bank of the St. Lawrence, to cheer us on in the fight!

He followed with a quote from Byron:

Freedom's battle, once begun,
Bequeathed from bleeding sire to son.
Though baffled oft, is always won.

What Happened to Lieutenant Johnson's Body?

During the night of November 13, Hunters stripped the uniform and sword from the body of Lieutenant William Johnson. Lyman Leach took the sword and presented it to Colonel von Schoultz, who awarded it to Captain Heustis. The uniform disappeared. To these facts, Heustis and other Hunters agreed.

That night, someone or something mutilated Lieutenant Johnson's corpse. Canadian and British sources claim that American raiders did the dirty deed. American sources claim hogs wandering the village fed on the body. This is backed up in Heustis's memoirs. At his trial, Von Schoultz denied any involvement in the atrocity and later claimed he had the offending pigs shot.

In the memoirs of Lieutenant Charles Parker, he blamed the indignities to Lieutenant Johnson's body on the Americans. However, he did record the presence of hogs near Johnson's body the first day, and he observed hogs eating corpses during his visit the day following the battle.

Windmill Battle, Day Two

The morning of Wednesday, November 14, 1838, dawned cold, windy and clear. The wet snow that covered the bodies the day before had hardened to icy coffins. Shortly after dawn, the three British gunboats returned and lobbed eighteen-pound balls of iron into Newport. A field gun north of the village added to the metal hail. Together, they did little damage. Both armies traded gun shots, more to stifle boredom than for military value.

Midmorning, new companies of militia joined the Newport cordon. On orders from Lieutenant Colonel Plomer Young, they fired on the outer ranks of Hunters, forcing them closer to the stone buildings. This allowed two officers a closer view.

One was Lieutenant Colonel Henry Dundas, commander of the British Eighty-third Regiment of Foot. The second was Major Forbes Macbean, an artillery expert. As a test, the *Cobourg* fired at the windmill. As usual, the cannonball bounced off. Dundas and Macbean concluded they needed much heavier ordnance. They returned to Kingston to arrange for it.

That morning, Captain Heustis relates that a band of Canadian militia overran a stone house on the periphery of Newport and began sniping at the Hunters. In response, Colonel von Schoultz led eleven men to retake the house. The Hunters drove off the enemy, set the house on fire and returned with two wounded prisoners.

Colonel Richard Fraser called a truce midmorning so that both sides could recover the dead. Von Schoultz agreed, and for an hour combatants politely helped each other pry bodies from their wintry tombs.

During the brief peace, von Schoultz asked to speak to Colonel Fraser. Historians speculate that the Hunter commander wanted to discuss terms of surrender. The bad-tempered Fraser refused to speak to him. To Fraser, von Schoultz was a brigand aligned with Bill Johnston, worthy only of hanging and not treatment as a gentleman.

For the rest of the day, the Hunters fortified their positions by blocking windows and doors with stone blocks. They entered these fortresses by ladders to second-story windows. Heustis related that his men behaved in good spirits. He singled out Garret Hicks, forty-five, a farmer from Alexandria, Jefferson County, who amused them for hours with humorous dog stories.

In contrast to Hicks's high spirits, one young raider named Hunter Vaughan, nineteen, from Sackets Harbor, strolled in solitude by the river. Once a fervent Patriot and recruiter for the Hunter army, he stood forlorn and disillusioned, gazing out at the American steamer *Telegraph*. His father, William Vaughan, captained that ship, and it was his duty to prevent anyone on the American side from bringing aid to his son and his comrades. Witnesses saw Hunter feebly wave a white handkerchief at the passing vessel.

Another snowstorm struck that night. Without candles, lamps or firewood, the Hunters shivered through the long, tenebrous night in complete darkness.

WINDMILL BATTLE, DAY THREE

Thursday morning, November 15, 1838, dawned cold and clear. No cannon barrage greeted the sunrise. The *Experiment* patrolled alone. Desultory sniping from both sides punctuated the morning's restless peace.

One incident that day perked up the Hunters' spirits. Heustis related how a British artillery squad tried to move a field gun closer to Newport that afternoon with a team of horses. A Hunter gunner fired a round from their six-pounder. The cannonball arched over the village and hit its target, killing one horse and smashing the whiffletree. The other horses bolted; the cannon flipped over, and its crew retreated.

Unbeknownst to the men trapped at Newport, prominent American citizens in Ogdensburg, including U.S. colonel William Jenkins Worth, met that morning to discuss ways of rescuing them. Worth proposed a meeting with Lieutenant Colonel Plomer Young. A man who knew Young crossed the river to Prescott with the invitation. Young agreed and met Worth on board the *Telegraph* mid-river.

In order to prevent further bloodshed, Worth proposed to Young that the Hunters be allowed to return to America. In return, he promised to lay charges against them in the United States, and American authorities vouched to prevent further rebel raids from northern New York. While Young sympathized with Worth's position, he explained that he risked severe military sanction and probably court-martial if he let the enemy escape.

In the conversation, Young told Worth that the big British gunboats had sailed to Kingston and that the *Experiment* intended to return to Prescott for maintenance. History does not tell us if Young let this military secret slip inadvertently or by design. Young wished Worth well and departed.

Worth seized the opportunity. He berthed the *Telegraph* in Ogdensburg and released the ferry steamer *Paul Pry* from impoundment. He organized a group of citizens, led by a member of the state assembly, Preston King, thirty-two, to undertake the actual rescue.

The *Experiment* returned to Prescott in mid-afternoon. On cue, the *Paul Pry* hurried from Ogdensburg and anchored offshore near the besieged

Preston King, 1855, the Ogdensburg postmaster who tried to rescue trapped Hunters in November 1838. *Library of Congress.*

windmill. One man, identified only as a Hunters Lodge member, volunteered to land and speak with Colonel von Schoultz.

That man falsely told von Schoultz that he had two choices: escape on the *Paul Pry* or wait for six hundred reinforcements in the morning. Perhaps because of lack of sleep and food, or a monumental ego, von Schoultz chose to wait for the phantom reinforcements. Hearing von Schoultz's decision, King rowed ashore and pleaded with the Hunter colonel to cast away any notion of fresh troops. In the end, all King received was a promise from von Schoultz to allow the wounded to board the *Paul Pry*.

King took one slightly wounded man with him to the steamer, while von Schoultz's men went to fetch others. When the *Paul Pry* tried to come closer, Canadian militiamen fired on it. The shots alerted Lieutenant William Fowell, and he steamed out in the *Experiment*, its repairs finished ahead of schedule. The *Paul Pry* fled to U.S. waters.

Gathering clouds dumped snow and sleet. For three hours, Hunters both wounded and well huddled on the stony beach in the foul cold hoping for the *Paul Pry*'s return.

Stephen Wright, in his memoirs, wrote that once it was evident the ferry would not return, "our fortunes grew desperate; the last glimmer of hope went out." Wright also lamented that if the *Paul Pry* had removed the wounded, the fit Hunters, relieved of their obligation to protect their comrades, could have smashed through the thin line of guards and fled into the countryside.

According to Captain Heustis, two Hunters found a canoe that evening and asked him to leave with them. The idealistic Hunter captain refused, saying he would not forsake the men he had led into harm's way. He wished the men well. They found a third volunteer and paddled to America only hours ahead of the final assault.

Windmill Battle, Day Four

On Friday, November 16, 1838, just 117 Hunters remained fit to fight. Hungry, cold, sleep deprived and disillusioned, they prepared for the final clash they knew they could not win. The trapped men huddled in their stone prisons as the force of regulars and Canadian militia surrounding their stronghold steadily grew.

Lieutenant Colonel Dundas brought three hundred seasoned infantry of the British Eighty-third Regiment of Foot. Lieutenant Colonel Young assembled at least six hundred of his citizen soldiers. A company from the Ninety-third Regiment of Foot, composed of battle-hardened Highlanders, joined the swelling army. Captain Williams Sandom packed the river with a fleet of gunboats towing barges with additional artillery.

The Hunters' biggest threat came from Major Forbes Macbean and his artillery squads. Early that day, he landed two massive cannons at

This twenty-four-pound cannon at Fort Henry resembles the eighteen-pounders fired the last day of the Battle of the Windmill. *Photo by the author.*

Prescott and had the 7,300-pound weapons hauled by teams of horses to a position four hundred yards north of the windmill. Macbean's men spent hours digging in the ordnance and readying the powder and eighteen-pound iron cannonballs. Unlike the carronades on Sandom's ships and the lighter field guns, Macbean's weapons were long-range building smashers. Colonel Nils von Schoultz, a former artillery officer in Europe, probably guessed what was in store for them.

At 1:00 p.m., Lieutenant Colonel Dundas sent a flag of truce to request an hour to remove the last bodies. Von Schoultz agreed and returned Canadian captives taken two days earlier. At their meeting in mid-battlefield, von Schoultz offered to surrender to prevent further bloodshed if Dundas

Though the naval carronades and Macbean's cannon all shot eighteen-pound balls, the cannon's longer barrel allowed the projectiles to reach higher speeds before exiting the muzzle. Greater speed meant a longer range and greater mass on contact.

pledged to treat the Hunters as prisoners of war. Dundas denied the request, saying that he'd accept only an unconditional surrender. Von Schoultz refused.

The *Telegraph*, with Colonel Worth onboard, patrolled in mid-river to prevent any Hunters or sympathetic Americans from aiding the besieged Hunters. This infuriated Captain Heustis. He berated his government as hypocritical and cowardly:

> *When Texas rebelled against the government of Mexico, thousands of American citizens crossed the lines and assisted in achieving her independence. They went and returned, as they pleased, without molestation from the government of the United States. Yet the contest in Texas was not so much a struggle for freedom as that in Canada.*
>
> *…every possible exertion has been made by the United States authorities to thwart and defeat us. In view of the outrageous insults we had received, as a nation, from the British Tories in Canada, we did think this extreme vigilance on the part of the United States government, in harassing the friends of Canadian liberty, altogether unworthy of republican America. Had* [any other nation] *perpetrated an outrage equal in enormity to the burning of the* Caroline, *even though provoked to it by flagrant acts of wrong on our part, the whole naval and military force of the country would have been in readiness to avenge the insult! But, in this case, troops were sent to the frontier, not to punish our insatiate foe, but to assist her in crushing the republican spirit which threatened to uproot British power in Canada!*

At 3:00 p.m., gunnery on Sandom's seven vessels and barges began the final bombardment of Newport. A half hour later, Macbean fired the first shot from one of his massive weapons. The eighteen-pound cannonball smacked into the windmill and deflected off, leaving the tower unscathed once more. The next shot from the second big gun caved in the nearest stone house, sending Hunters running.

Macbean's experienced artillery crews fired each gun every two minutes. They steadily dismantled Newport as every shot hit its target. Sandom's fleet and fifteen lighter field cannons also rained iron on the hamlet to keep the Hunter snipers pinned down. It worked. They fired only occasional shots that afternoon.

The three Hunter guns had exhausted their meager supply of cannonballs. The gunners resorted to using scrap iron. Occasionally, the

Hunters retrieved a used six-pound ball from a British gun, loaded it up and fired it back.

At dusk that short November day, the Hunters occupied just two structures. The majority huddled in the windmill. A dozen or so Hunters defended the stone tavern. Snipers lurked in the ruins of other buildings.

Minutes ahead of the final Canadian troop assault, the Hunter officers gathered at the tavern. Colonels Dorephus Abbey and Martin Woodruff wanted to surrender. Colonel Nils von Schoultz and Captain Daniel Heustis refused. Woodruff returned to the windmill. Abbey quietly exited the tavern, walked to the Canadian lines and surrendered.

The hot-headed Colonel Richard Fraser spotted Abbey. He rode over on horseback and smacked Abbey's buttocks with the flat of his sword. Abbey dropped to his knees in intense stinging pain.

At 4:30 p.m., Dundas ordered his army to advance on the Hunters. Macbean ceased firing to avoid hitting his own men.

The British regulars methodically advanced, setting fire to each building to drive out any Hunters. As the unstoppable wall of death closed in on the center of Newport, Captain Heustis and Colonel Woodruff marched from the windmill under a white flag. A squad of Canadian militia ignored the surrender notice and fired at them, sending them scurrying to the windmill.

Captain Sandom witnessed that dishonorable event. A man of unimpeachable honor, he ordered his marines to shoot any militiaman who fired on a truce flag again.

Sandom sent Lieutenant George Leary under a flag of truce to the windmill. He brought back Captain Christopher Buckley to parlay with Captain Sandom and Lieutenant Colonel Dundas. On spotting Buckley, Colonel Fraser rode over on horseback and laid his trademark sword spanking on Buckley. Ignoring Sandom's protests, Fraser trotted off.

Buckley limped back to the windmill. Its occupants surrendered unconditionally and marched out between two lines of British regulars, who protected the Hunters from militiamen who wanted no quarter given.

At the tavern, von Schoultz told his men to give up or flee as they chose. Militiamen bayoneted two men who walked out with their hands up.

Von Schoultz fled into the dark with Hunter Vaughan and others. Scouts captured the colonel within two hours and Vaughan after two days. Several men found unguarded boats and returned to America. Heustis listed the successful escapees as "Jonah Woodruff, William Hathaway, Benjamin Fulton, Tracy (unknown first name) and a Polander," whose name he could not recall. It is likely that the Pole slipped through the lines

This watercolor by Henry Francis Ainslie, 1839, shows the desolation of Newport after the Battle of the Windmill in 1838.

dressed in the uniform taken earlier from Lieutenant William Johnson's corpse. A man calling himself Nathan Williams later claimed he escaped on the last day.

Von Schoultz's captors hauled him before the victorious commander, Lieutenant Colonel Dundas. In the imperious tones of an upper-class Englishman, he excoriated his captive for attacking a peaceful country. Von Schoultz reportedly shrugged and replied, "I am a soldier. I undertook to hold a certain post. I defended it to the last. You would not think the better of me for being a coward."

The battle over, the surviving Hunters plodded to Prescott guarded by the Eighty-third Regiment of Foot. The next day, they boarded ships for the prisons of Fort Henry in Kingston. Troops searched each man for military information. Heustis wrote that his coat contained two letters from Bill Johnston that they thankfully missed. Heustis ditched them at the first opportunity.

Newport lay in ruins, its roofless homes open to the winter elements, its grounds pockmarked with craters and its grove of butternut trees smashed. The inhabitants did not return to rebuild.

Thirty years later, author and artist Benson Lossing sketched the village, still in ruins. Only the indomitable windmill survived.

How Many Really Died?

The count of Hunters killed and captured varies among sources. By comparing lists, the British probably captured 161 Hunters, including 17 wounded, of which 3 died. Heustis's memoir lists 17 men who died during the battle. (Some sources state that 50 Hunters died, but no list of Hunter participants supports that number.)

That so few Hunters died in four days of bombardment is a testament to von Schoultz's defensive strategy and the thick stone buildings of poor little Newport.

The official count of thirteen Canadian and British troops killed and sixty-nine wounded seems suspiciously low. Historian Donald E. Graves lists seventeen deaths from the four-day engagement. Eyewitness accounts suggest a much greater toll. We do know that bodies so littered the battlefield that it took a truce on the second and fourth days to remove them all.

William Gates wrote that on the first day he "saw some twenty acres almost literally covered with the fallen" and nine wagons piled with enemy bodies "not numbering less than three hundred."

Stephen Wright estimated the enemy casualties at between four and six hundred. He added, "I distinctly recollect seeing from the top of the mill, a vehicle drawn by four horses, engaged in collecting the enemies' dead during the engagement. There must have been two hundred wounded."

Daniel Heustis wrote, "The loss of the enemy was stated on our trial, by a government witness, to have been 20 officers, and upwards of 300 men, killed, and a large number wounded." (The existing transcript of his trial does not include casualty figures.)

Though the Hunters certainly exaggerated their estimates, by any account, the Battle of the Windmill was the deadliest encounter for Canadian forces in the Patriot War.

15

Trials and Hangings Follow Capture of Hunters

November–December 1838

During the Battle of the Windmill, Bill Johnston tried to reverse his first day's efforts. Twice, he scoured the town in a vain effort to encourage men to take small boats across and bring the trapped Hunters home. It tore at him cruelly to be safe while friends and compatriots faced peril. He tried to get across on Wednesday night, November 14, but could not breach the blockade. What was worse, people called him a coward behind his back for not being in the fight. Wind went out of his mighty sails that week.

The Hunter defeat at Newport and months of hiding from the law had depleted Bill's hardy spirit. He hatched a scheme with his son John to give himself up, but an eager deputy marshal ruined his plans on November 17.

Historical accounts vary on the actual circumstances of Bill Johnston's arrest. Benson Lossing, in his book *Pictorial Field-Book of the War of 1812*, tells the story based on an interview with Bill about 1869:

> He saw that all was lost, and, weary of hiding, he resolved to give himself up to the authorities of the United States, and cast himself upon the clemency of his country. He made an arrangement with his son John to arrest him and receive the $500 reward. On the 17th of November, he left for Ogdensburg in a boat with his son, when Deputy Marshal McCulloch pursued him in a boat over which floated the revenue flag. Johnston was overtaken about two miles above Ogdensburg. He was armed with a Cochran rifle, two large rifle-pistols, and a bowie-knife.

(A Cochran rifle is an early multi-round rifle.)

This lithograph, from the memoirs of Daniel Heustis, depicts the Battle of the Windmill as Bill Johnston would have seen it from Ogdensburg.

According to historian John Northman, when men in McCulloch's posse grabbed Bill, he shook them off and then leveled his pistols ready for a fight. But he hesitated, not wanting to kill fellow Americans. Instead, he and John negotiated surrender, and Bill gave his weapons to his son.

McCulloch took Johnston to Ogdensburg and delivered him to Colonel Worth. He imprisoned Johnston on the *Telegraph* with other captives, including John Ward Birge, the Hunter general; William Sprague, captain of the Hunter ship *Charlotte of Oswego*; and Isaac Tiffany, the gunner who helped fire a field gun at the *Experiment* the first day of the battle.

U.S. marshal Nathaniel Garrow, fifty-eight, took the accused by steamer and train to Cayuga, New York, where townsfolk cheered their arrival, and then on to nearby Auburn for trial. Rather than placing his charges in jail, Garrow lodged them in rooms near his in the American Hotel with guards at the doors.

On Friday, November 23, guards assembled the prisoners for a preliminary hearing on charges that they contravened the U.S. Neutrality Act. Judge Alfred Conklin, New York circuit judge for the northern district, held them over for trial on November 28. Isaac Tiffany had no stomach for a trial and fled jail on the twenty-sixth.

The trial acquitted Bill Johnston because no evidence proved he was involved in the Battle of the Windmill. The marshal promptly arrested him on an outstanding warrant related to the Hickory Island affair in February 1838.

Late that night, Johnston and Birge (who had not been acquitted) slipped from their shared hotel room past three guards and vanished into the night. Garrow posted a $200 reward for Admiral Johnston and a mere $50 for General Birge.

Bill always said that no prison could hold him if he chose not to stay.

Where Is Bill Johnston's Portrait?

During Johnston's short stay in Auburn, Randall Palmer, thirty-one, a locally famous artist, offered to paint his portrait. That Palmer usually painted high society figures, such as the Van Rensselaer clan, must have impressed Johnston.

Accounts describe the painting as forty inches high by fifty inches wide, with small river scenes painted in the margins. The Rochester *Democrat*'s editor wrote a review in 1839:

> The result is a most striking likeness of the bold buccaneer. He is "long-favored"—with features spare, yet prominent and bold. There is in his eye a perceptible shrewdness, which makes him a man of quick comprehension—stern and resolute. He holds in his hand a spy glass, and in the perspective is seen a boat propelled by a female intending to represent Miss Johnston… [this picture] will secure to the Commodore a canvass existence long after tyranny shall have been driven from the Canadas…a copy of this portrait is to be sent to Johnston's family.

The two portraits of Bill Johnston are harder to locate than their subject was in the Thousand Islands in 1838. Both disappeared without a trace. For decades, one copy hung in the ornate staircase in the Carnegie-era public library in Syracuse. It disappeared when the library relocated its central collection in 1988.

TRIALS BEGIN FOR CAPTURED HUNTER OFFICERS

Following the bloody Battle of the Windmill, the Canadian colonial public wanted blood in return, and the Upper Canada government eagerly prepared to give it to them. Four days after the smoke cleared, Lieutenant Governor Sir George Arthur laid the groundwork for mass trials in Kingston. The colony's solicitor general, Lieutenant Colonel William Draper, thirty-seven, took charge as judge advocate with the goal to try all prisoners before the end of December 1838. With that schedule, Draper allowed almost no time for the accused to prepare a defense.

The windmill captives faced charges under the Lawless Aggressions Act. Draper had no intention of using a civilian jury, as with the Short Hills raiders, where sympathies could not be controlled. The windmill prisoners faced a military court-martial whose members were openly hostile to the American raiders.

In Draper's one concession to justice, he allowed prisoners to ask questions of any witness, though the act required no such privilege. Most accused did not use that opportunity.

Four captured Hunters (three Canadians and one American) agreed to become state witnesses in exchange for clemency. Canadian Levi Chipman, forty-five, an early Hunter recruit, turned out to be Draper's best resource when he needed to establish a man's participation in the Newport raid.

William Gates wrote that a prosecutor offered him clemency if he became a witness for the queen. He told them, "I choose death with my fellows rather than life at their expense."

The pending trials became the talk of Kingston—an unparalleled news event. Into the limelight stepped John A. Macdonald, twenty-three, an upstart local lawyer. In July, he had successfully defended eight men arrested and accused of treason. This time, he agreed to defend Hunter officers Nils von Schoultz, thirty-one; Daniel George, twenty-seven; and Dorephus Abbey, forty-seven.

Macdonald took a professional risk defending the Hunters because the colony so reviled the raiders, but he believed all men had a right to justice. He also faced enormous legal roadblocks. The Lawless Aggressions Act prevented Macdonald from openly defending his clients in court; he could only coach them on how to manage their own defense.

Daniel George faced court-martial on Wednesday, November 28, 1838, in front of sixteen officers in dress uniforms at Fort Henry. Guards lined the wall. The Onondaga Hunters' flag taken from the windmill hung on the wall. A pile of confiscated guns and Bowie knives lay on display, giving silent testimony.

George's trial consumed all that day and the morning of the next. Being the initial case, Draper was thorough in laying out the evidence. George claimed he was out for a row to watch the fighting. (He was arrested trying to escape in a small boat the first day.) Chipman testified to George's real role as paymaster and troop leader. Also, the court-martial heard that guards had found receipts in George's pockets from the captain of the *United States* for towing the two rebel schooners on November 11. The court pronounced him guilty.

Von Schoultz's short trial began the same day, November 29. From the start, any defense was impossible. The Hunter colonel took full responsibility for the assault on Newport. He confessed that he had invaded Upper Canada in a complete misunderstanding of the inhabitants' real circumstances and admitted he was culpable and should pay for his crimes. Draper warned the colonel that a guilty plea meant execution. Von Schoultz remained resolute. He asked only that the authorities to be merciful to his men. The court convicted him.

Von Schoultz never denied his guilt; he accepted his fate, and he stoically prepared for death. His bravery and sense of honor in the face of certain execution did not go unnoticed. The following appeared in the *Oswego Palladium* on December 12, 1838:

> *As an indication of how Von Schoultz impressed his captors and how they came to regard him, it is worthy of mention that officers of the British army stationed at Kingston after Von Schoultz['s] conviction, which automatically carried with it a sentence of death, signed a petition addressed to the governor of Upper Canada requesting that executive clemency should be extended in this case.*

Macdonald prepared a will for von Schoultz. The colonel bequeathed £400 to widows of British soldiers killed during the battle and another sum to a Roman Catholic college being built in Kingston. Macdonald refused to accept legal fees.

Von Schoultz wrote farewell letters to friends, such as the following one to Warren Green in Syracuse:

> *Dear Friend—When you get this letter, I shall be no more. I have been informed that my execution will take place tomorrow. May God forgive them who brought me to this untimely death. Hard as my fate is, I have made up*

my mind to forgive them, and do. I have been promised a lawyer to write my will—intend to appoint you my executor. If the British government permits it, I wish my body delivered to you and buried on your farm. I have no time to write more because I have great need of communicating with my Creator to prepare myself for His presence. The time allowed me for this is short. My last wish to the Americans is that they will not think of avenging my death. Let no further blood be shed. And believe me, from what I have seen, all the stories which were told of the sufferings of the Canadian people were untrue. Give my love to your sister, and tell her that I think of her as I do of my own mother. May God reward her for her kindness. Farewell, my dear friends. May God bless you and protect you.

Dorephus Abbey

Any history of early newspapers in upstate New York includes the name Dorephus Abbey. Born in Suffield, Connecticut, he became a printer and then a newspaper publisher.

In 1815, he and his brother Seth started a monthly paper, the *Friend*. In 1817, the Abbey brothers opened the weekly *Jefferson and Lewiston Gazette*. It continued until April 1819. Seth went on to start other newspapers, while Dorephus helped found the *Oswego Palladium*. Dorephus resigned from that paper once it was well established and purchased the *Republican Herald* in Binghamton, New York, in 1820.

He married Catherine Clark of Herkimer, New York. They had a son and two daughters. About 1837, he retired from newspapers and became a farmer in Jefferson County.

A letter in the *Watertown Herald* on August 19, 1893, from one William Fayel, discussed people he'd met during the Patriot War:

> *I knew Dorephus Abbey, who lived on Hyde Lake, and came to Hiram Becker's "Old Red Tavern" on the Military Road where I saw him. He had been the editor of a paper in Albany and had just sold out, when the Hunters Lodge took him in. He was a fine intelligent gentleman.*

At forty-six, Abbey forsook the newspaperman's credo "the pen is mightier than the sword" when he joined the Hunters in the summer of 1838 and then became a colonel in Birge's army.

Abbey faced his accusers on November 30, 1838. He followed Macdonald's guidance, insisting he was an unwilling participant in the battle, essentially kidnapped and forced to fight. Levi Chipman's evidence shot holes in the story. The court-martial convicted and sentenced Abbey that day.

On December 11, 1838, he wrote farewell letters to his children, who would soon be orphans (their mother died in 1837). To his son, Clark, he gave words of encouragement, including:

> *Arm yourself my dear boy with fortitude, to hear the sad intelligence, that ere these lines meet your eye, I am numbered with the dead. My zeal in the cause of universal freedom has eventually cost me my life…As regards yourself, cultivate your mind, associate with honorable men, aim high and let all your motives be of an exalted character; and now, my beloved son, I bid you adieu forever.*

To his daughters, Amelia and Arabella, he spoke of their future and his dim present:

> *Many severe trials have awaited you from your earliest childhood, but that which you have now to endure, will require all your firmness; you are now left without a parent. Tomorrow morning closes my earthly senses.*

He named two family friends who promised to look out for their welfare and closed with:

> *I write from a gloomy cell, lying upon a bed of straw; the guard will soon call for the light, and I must close. Since my sentence, I could not procure materials for writing, till this late hour of my existence, which have just been furnished me by direction of the sheriff. Present me kindly to kindred and friends. I cannot discriminate; so farewell, my dear children.*

VON SCHOULTZ HANGED

December 8, 1838, dawned cool and hazy—a common climate by Lake Ontario in that season. At 8:00 a.m., soldiers transported von Schoultz by wagon from the Kingston jail to the plateau next to Fort Henry. There waited a special gallows built just for him. That and the dress uniform von

This watercolor by Henry Francis Ainslie, 1839, shows the gallows erected beside Fort Henry to hang Nils von Schoultz. *Library and Archives Canada, C-000510.*

Schoultz wore were concessions to his rank. Those minor privileges may also be attributable to the respect von Schoultz had garnered among the military for his honesty and gallantry.

Lieutenant Charles Parker attended the execution and noted details in his memoirs. Two priests accompanied von Schoultz to the scaffold, where he knelt and said a short prayer. While the sheriff read the warrant for his execution, the colonel gave last instructions to a priest. The hangmen put the cord over his head, placed a cap over his eyes and tied his hands, but so loosely that von Schoultz adjusted the noose himself. The hangmen pulled the bolt on the trapdoor. Von Schoultz fell, convulsed three times, trembled and was still.

Another eyewitness account of his last hour comes from a seven-year-old boy named William Allen, who lived across from the Kingston jail on Wellington Street. As an adult, Allen wrote:

> *The morning Von Schoultz was to be hanged I was ordered to keep at home, but I got out, attracted by the soldiers. They were about the jail. Von Schoultz came out attended by two priests, one on each side of him. He was placed in a cart and the company proceeded to the fort. Boy-like, I followed*

and was soon trudging along with the soldiers across the bridge and up the fort hill. When the gallows was reached…an upright post with an arm and a rope…the cart drove under the arm, the rope was adjusted, the prayers said, and then the cart drove ahead, leaving the man dangling from the rope.

The witness accounts vary on the method of hanging. Parker described a trapdoor, and Allen said a cart pulled away. Hangmen aimed for a quick kill, if possible, so the trapdoor is more likely the accurate account because the fall breaks the victim's neck.

The day Colonel von Schoultz died, Sheriff Macdonell took Dorephus Abbey and Daniel George from the fort to Kingston's jail to wait for their date with the hangman. Abbey shook the hand of each man in the casement and bid each farewell. In his memoirs, Heustis revealed his poetic heart:

There is a melting power in that single word "farewell"—when spoken for the last time, under such peculiar and distressing circumstances—which opens the fountain of the heart, and sends tears of sorrow trickling down the hardy cheeks of manhood.

On December 12, Abbey and George dropped through the gallows' trapdoor at the Kingston jail. Daniel Heustis summed up the prisoners' fears, angers and uncertainties:

The reign of terror had now commenced. We were in the hands of the Robespierres of Canada, and the guillotine was in readiness to dispatch its victims. The gloom and monotony of prison life; the unrelenting murder of our beloved commander, the uncertainty which brooded over our destiny; the bloodthirsty disposition evinced by the Tories, and especially by Governor Arthur, to whom we were obliged to look for clemency; the summary process of trying us by a court-martial, composed of persons known to be violently hostile to us, and selected for that very reason; the effort to induce some of our men to turn Queen's witnesses, by an offer of free pardon for themselves—all these things tended to render our situation exceedingly unpleasant.

It was boldly declared, in advance of any trial, that all the leaders, at least, would be hung. How comprehensive the Tory definition of the word "leaders" might be, we had no very satisfactory means of deciding.

HUNTER PRISONERS TRIED IN GROUPS

Following the single trials of Nils von Schoultz, Daniel George and Dorephus Abbey, the Upper Canada court-martial machine shifted into high gear. The colony's solicitor general, Lieutenant Colonel William Henry Draper, tried the windmill raiders in groups ranging in number from three to twelve.

Prisoners filed in between rows of guards and stood facing a table of officers, plus Draper. As judge advocate, Draper acted as the Crown's representative and ran the trials, but it was the officers—representing the infantry, navy, artillery and militia—who judged the defendants. A guilty verdict required a two-thirds majority of officers. Trial deliberations were brief, and in most cases, the penalty was death.

On December 3, 1838, Colonel Martin Woodruff, William Gates and three others were the first men tried as a group. As with previous trials, Draper relied heavily on the testimony of the turncoat Levi Chipman. The court-martial convicted all five and sentenced them to death.

On December 5, Draper tried eleven prisoners at once. On December 10, he tried twelve more, including Hunter Vaughan. All were found guilty and sentenced to hang.

Despite the crowded docket, the trials did not last long, and access to witnesses was severely curtailed, as Stephen Wright detailed in his memoirs. On December 22, Wright and eleven others faced the court-martial. He complained in court that, having just heard the charges, they needed time to procure witnesses:

> I told the Judge Advocate, George Draper, that I thought it was unjust to be tried for our lives and not be allowed time to procure witnesses. He answered "they would do no good," and I thought he was angry at my remark. I then said "the proceedings of the court-martial are more like condemning than trying the prisoners." At which he called me an insolent, impertinent scoundrel, and he then proceeded to business. We were all tried and convicted, including the examination of one witness, in twenty-eight minutes, in a very summary manner.

Just twenty-eight minutes to find twelve men guilty of a hanging offense mocked hundreds of years of British jurisprudence. The conviction machine devised and staged by Draper dispensed revenge, not justice. Gates confirms in his memoirs that the group trials were brief:

In a similar manner were all our comrades tried, often a dozen or fifteen at a batch, whilst the whole time occupied, from the moment they left the room till their return to it again, would not exceed generally over one hour. All that seemed necessary was to bring the culprit into the presence of the court to hear his indictment, and to give him the opportunity of repeating "Guilty" or "Not Guilty" either of which was sufficient to warrant a condemnation.

CAPTAIN VAUGHAN HUNTS DOWN BILL JOHNSTON

After Bill Johnston escaped custody on November 28, 1838, one man made it his mission to track down the fugitive and apprehend him by whatever means possible. Few men had the skills and daring to find, corner and confront Johnston, but this pursuer was Johnston's equal.

As a steamship skipper, Captain William Vaughan knew the Thousand Islands as well as Johnston. As a young naval officer, Vaughan was an ally of Johnston's during the War of 1812. Together, they had raided British supply ships. When the British captured Vaughan's son Hunter following the windmill battle, Vaughan held Johnston at least partly responsible.

Sketch of Captain William Vaughan by Benson Lossing from his book *Pictorial Field-Book of the War of 1812*, 1869.

On December 8, an informant told Vaughan that he saw Bill Johnston in Salina (near Syracuse, New York). Bill had left Salina when Vaughan arrived. Based on a tip, Vaughan set out alone in a sleigh on December 10 for a forty-six-mile journey through the early winter countryside. His destination was a farm near the small town of Rome, where Vaughan heard Johnston was staying with family. (Relatives of Bill's wife, Ann, lived near Rome.)

Vaughan walked unannounced into the farmhouse at 9:00 p.m. and demanded that Johnston return to Salina with him. Though armed with pistols and a dirk, Bill gave no resistance. Vaughan and his prisoner arrived at Salina at six o'clock the next morning, where Vaughan handed Johnston to a deputy marshal.

From there, the three men journeyed to Syracuse, where Johnston again found himself in the custody of U.S. marshal Nathaniel Garrow. Two days later, Garrow escorted Johnston into a prison cell in Albany.

On December 14, the *Albany Evening Journal* published a letter supposedly written by Johnston from prison. He denied that he helped plan the raid on Prescott. Further, he stated that he tried to dissuade the leaders against it because he believed they had insufficient men, ammunition and experienced officers and would hang if captured. The letter's last paragraph showed his frustration at the poor state of the Patriot movement and specific but unnamed persons:

> *The Patriot cause has suffered and is still suffering more from pretended friends in the States than from its open enemies in Canada. It is from the treachery of a pretended Patriot that your humble servant is within the walls of this prison.*

People vilified Captain Vaughan as a traitor to Bill Johnston. But Vaughan's efforts paid off. In gratitude for the capture of Johnston, the colonial government pardoned Hunter Vaughan and shipped him home that spring.

Bill Johnston settled in to spend the winter in prison.

CAPTAIN DANIEL HEUSTIS TRIED

Each court-martial of Hunters under the Lawless Aggressions Act mocked justice, even by the heavy-handed British standards of the time. It permitted few avenues of defense and allowed the feeblest evidence to stand as fact. The court-martial of Daniel Heustis, Orrin W. Smith and ten others on December 17, 1838, provides an example.

Draper swore in the judging officers and read the long-winded charges. With minor modifications (dates and names of accused), the following words match the indictment read to all accused Hunters:

> *On the 12th day of November, and on divers other days between that day and the 16th day of November, in the second year of the reign of our Sovereign Lady Victoria, by the Grace of God ruler of the United Kingdom of Great Britain and defender of the faith, with force and arms at the township of Edwardsburg in the Province of Upper Canada, being citizens of foreign states at peace with the United Kingdom, that is to say, the United States of America, having joined themselves to divers subjects of said Lady the Queen, who were then and there unlawfully and traitorously in arms against our said Lady the Queen, [list of defendants' names] did then and there make war on our said Lady the Queen, armed with guns, bayonets and other warlike weapons, and did kill and slay divers of her Majesty's loyal subjects.*

When asked to plea, every captive replied not guilty.

To convict an American prisoner, Draper had to prove three things: that the accused was a citizen of a foreign country at peace with England, that he conspired with British subjects bearing arms against the queen and that he actively participated in the hostilities. For the queen's subjects, the rules were similar. A conviction meant a death sentence regardless of nationality.

Draper called Christopher Armstrong, a barrister, to the stand. He had previously interviewed the inmates and recorded each man's age, occupation and country of origin. Armstrong testified that each accused present that day claimed to be a United States citizen. That meant that Draper had passed the first test of a successful prosecution, even though, technically, the Americans had unknowingly borne witness against themselves.

Draper next called a sergeant of the Eighty-third Regiment who witnessed the Hunters surrender at the windmill. He assured the court that the men captured that day were the same men imprisoned in the fort.

Draper's next witness, Ensign William Nott, described the weapons recovered at Newport.

Two barristers, George Barker and William McKay, who had previously interviewed the Hunters, read statements of facts given by the prisoners. While supposedly part of each man's defense, the barristers' testimony was far from impartial.

In his memories, Heustis wrote that prisoners had to sign a statement "colored to their disadvantage" during the interviews. When he balked, the official said, "There is no need to be stubborn, you are sure to be hanged." And Heustis replied, "If the government has already decided to hang us, do not expect us to provide the rope."

Heustis's statement at his trial said:

Daniel D. Heustis. Native of Cheshire County, New Hampshire, laborer, aged twenty-seven, stated that he lately resided in Watertown and was sworn in as a Hunter in that place about the first of October last. On Sunday the eleventh of November, one thousand eight hundred and thirty-eight, joined with many others and embarked on the United States *at Sackets Harbor and was told that he would be landed at Ogdensburg—paid his passage, one dollar. On the same night was ordered onboard a schooner [that] ran aground and the prisoner was ordered to go aboard another that came along side, which he accordingly went and was landed at Windmill Point below Prescott. Was confined in the hold of the vessel. He refused going ashore but was told by Abbey that as soon as the other schooner could be got off the ground the vessel should come and take him away again to the American shore. On Monday morning, the prisoner was ordered into the mill and to take arms. He went into the mill but refused to take arms. There were guns within reach of him. [During] the battle on Tuesday the thirteenth—assisted in laying up close before the mill door. On Friday tried to escape but was told by von Schoultz that he would be shot if he should try it.*

Naval lieutenant George Leary next told the court that he had observed the final battle, witnessed the Hunters surrender and inspected stacks of arms and ammunition. He testified that any man captured that day was surely involved in the hostilities. Draper accepted that sweeping generality as evidence.

Heustis clearly lied to help his case. For one, he was thirty-two not twenty-seven. He probably thought a young man would be treated leniently.

Captain Edward Townsend of the Eighty-third Regiment said he had made a list of all captives brought to the fort after the surrender and testified that those in court that day were on that list.

146

The next witness, Lieutenant Charles Parker, described the first assault on Newport, the casualties his force suffered and the death of Lieutenant William Johnson. Draper asked him if there was general gunfire coming from the Hunters or if only parts of the Hunter force shot at the British. Parker replied that he believed the fire was of a general nature.

Draper should have limited testimony from Parker, a battle combatant and a casualty, to simple statements of fact. But Draper allowed Parker's tainted opinion into evidence.

By this point, Draper had proven to his satisfaction that each prisoner before him was a U.S. citizen and had been actively engaged in the fighting. Evidence of the latter was circumstantial but sufficed in this case. He now needed to prove that the accused had conspired with British subjects.

For that, he called Levi Chipman to testify. Levi admitted that he, his brother Truman and James Philips were citizens of Upper Canada and fought at the Siege of Newport. He then identified several defendants as men definitely involved in the hostilities, including stating that Heustis had carried a sword and talked with officers. Levi admitted that he could not confirm that all raiders in court that day had fought at the windmill.

That ended the prosecution.

Lastly, each prisoner read his own defense statement. Heustis spoke briefly:

> *We were ordered by Abbey on shore, who stated that the boat would come to take us away immediately. I cannot say I did not lay hold of a sword but it was not to use it. I would hope the court would consider that if we shall be found guilty, they will not impose death but some other punishment that we may have a chance to live better hereafter.*

In short order, Draper had met the three tests needed for a conviction. He proved that every accused man was an American engaged in the hostilities who conspired with one of Her Majesty's subjects (Chipman) to attack the colony. Even though Chipman did not positively identify all defendants, Draper extended Chipman's limited evidence to everyone. The fact that the testimony of the sergeant and officers amounted to hearsay evidence did not bother Draper.

Draper sent the men to the cells. The officers conferred briefly, found every defendant guilty and recommended the death penalty for all.

Hanging of Hunters Continues

Throughout December 1838, the Upper Canada solicitor general, Lieutenant Colonel William Draper, kept up the relentless pace of his show trials in Kingston. In concert, the ever-stolid Lieutenant Governor Sir George Arthur confirmed the execution orders that kept the town's hangmen busy.

A steady parade of American men, whom people in upstate New York viewed as freedom fighters, paid the ultimate price for their misguided heroics.

Colonel Martin Woodruff mounted the gallows on December 19—the last senior Hunter officer to hang. By all accounts, he fell into the hands of amateur hangmen that day. Woodruff—a big man, over six feet tall and well past two hundred pounds—dropped through the trapdoor and, in front of 250 witnesses, died an agonizing death.

In his memoirs, William Gates gave a second-hand account (verified by old newspaper reports) of Woodruff's last minutes:

> *The knot, instead of drawing tightly under the ear, slipped to the chin, leaving considerable space, and throwing the weight of the body upon the jack of the neck. In this manner he remained writhing in torment, till the spectators cried out for shame, when two hangmen stepped out and strove to strangle the poor sufferer! Failing in this, one ascended to the cross-bar, where, grasping the rope, he jerked the body upwards and downward, as he would have done a sheep-stealing dog, four successive times, before the neck was broken and the lamp of life extinguished in its mortal clay.*

Jefferson County residents Joel Peeler, forty-one, a farmer from Rutland, and Sylvanus Swete (aka Sweet), twenty-one, a cooper from Alexandria, faced their executions on December 22. Evidence against Swete stated that he was a sniper who killed Lieutenant William Johnson on the battle's first day. Peeler was accused of mutilating Johnson's corpse.

The sheriff always took men to the Kinston jail four days before a scheduled execution. In each instant, he entered the casement with guards, called out a man's name and made him stand at the room's center as he read the execution order. At one such visit from the sheriff, William Gates thought his turn had come:

> *"William Gates!" sounded in my ears, and falteringly I stood up. "Stand there," commanded the sheriff, pointing to the center of the room, as was his habit when about to read a death warrant. Seven other names were called,*

five of which were those of my room mates. He then read death warrants to those five. When turning and handing me a paper, he said, "Here, Gates, is a letter from your father; go and sit down." It was with great difficulty I regained a seat again. The revulsion of my feelings nearly overpowered me.

WHERE WERE THE EXECUTED BURIED?

Historical accounts suggest that colonial authorities buried most executed Hunters in unmarked graves, but newer evidence suggests otherwise. The current burial site of Nils von Schoultz and Martin Woodruff is well known, though the complete story of how they got there is not often told.

The British did not respect von Schoultz's last wish that his body be shipped to Syracuse. Instead, jailers buried him in a cemetery on Ordnance Street, then on the edge of Kingston. Called the Upper Burying Ground, it was shared by local churches and the garrison. Since a military court-martial condemned the men, burial in or near the garrison plot makes sense.

Tombstones of Martin Woodruff and Nils von Schoultz in St. Mary's Catholic Church cemetery, Kingston, Ontario. *Photo by the author.*

Jailers also initially interred Woodruff in the Upper Burying Ground. Friends shipped Dorephus Abbey's body to the Brookside Cemetery in Watertown, New York.

The Upper Burying Ground filled to capacity by the 1860s and became neglected and vandalized. Families and congregations transferred coffins to newer cemeteries. Engulfed by the growing town, the cemetery officially closed in the 1890s and was plowed over. It is now McBurney Park, unofficially known in Kingston as Skeleton Park.

For any executed American buried there, their grave markers disappeared long ago. Thanks to a Kingston tavern keeper, two survived. In 1862, Alexander Cicolari, an Italian Canadian born in Quebec who lived near the cemetery, had the bodies of von Schoultz and Woodruff moved to his family plot in Kingston's St. Mary's Cemetery.

Why spend money reburying strangers? At sixteen, Cicolari witnessed the hanging of von Schoultz and decided to honor his courage.

16

Trials End, Hangings Continue

January–February 1839

G uards locked up the captured windmill raiders in five of Fort Henry's stone casements normally used as barracks for enlisted men. Each room included barred windows at one end, a wood stove, a pile of firewood and a large tub for use as a toilet (emptied once a day).

William Gates described their lodgings in his memoirs:

> *The warmth of the room and its occupation by a large number of human beings, with the very slightest means of ventilation, rendered its atmosphere exceedingly disgusting and unwholesome; and add to this the tormenting annoyance of incredible numbers of vermin, and our situation, it may well be imagined, was debasing, and our treatment unchristian.*

All captives answered to Sheriff Allan Macdonell. A former British officer, he was appointed Midland District sheriff in March 1837. He acted as principal keeper and ombudsman for his charges. While as sheriff he arranged for any executions, he also stood up for the prisoners' limited rights.

On his instructions, each casement appointed a captain to keep order. All communications to the sheriff had to be made through the captains. The forty-two men in his casement elected Daniel Heustis as captain.

The first week, Macdonell allowed one man per casement to write a letter to friends or family. (Letter writing became a regular and unrestricted privilege.) On behalf of his group, Heustis wrote to Bernard Bagley in Watertown, New York, imploring him to send money so that

These upper and lower casements at Fort Henry housed the Hunters captured at the Battle of the Windmill. *Photo by the author.*

the prisoners could purchase better clothing and extra food. Bagley soon sent them $300.

Macdonell managed the inmates' money. He collected and pooled all funds sent by relatives and friends and distributed the cash, making sure every man received an equal portion to pay for straw mattresses, blankets, dishes, shaving utensils, knives and forks and anything else they wanted. That way, no man went without for lack of monied friends and family.

Macdonell kept detailed accounts, and there is no evidence that he used any funds for himself. Gates, who never had a good word to say about the sheriff, suspected some money lined Macdonell's pockets. Other prisoners trusted him immediately. In one of his parting letters to a friend, von Schoultz wrote:

> Some of the prisoners have already got an answer to their letters; money and clothing have been sent to them thro' the hands of the sheriff, who has appointed a man here in the fort, who attends to us; he has opened an account book for them, and buys every thing they wish for.

Some captives, frustrated with Macdonell's control of all funds, contrived to get money directly, as Heustis related:

> *Our friends from the United States were frequently over to see us, and by various stratagems we contrived to get in private money, with which, through the agency of the cook, we procured various little essential articles of comfort. By previous arrangement with their friends, some of the men received bank bills sewed up in clothing sent to them.*

Personal accounts of Macdonell by Hunter captives (some wrongly called him McDonald) remarked how he was cranky and profane but fair. Heustis wrote:

> *Sheriff McDonald [sic] was a large, stout, and good-looking Scotchman. He was a proud man, and was colonel of the Glengarry [militia] regiment. Prompt and faithful in the discharge of his duty as an officer, he was not destitute of humane feelings, and never insulted us, as did others, with ungentlemanly and abusive remarks, calculated to irritate and annoy us. He was in the habit of using quite too much profane language; in fact, he rarely spoke without introducing expressions that it would be improper for me to repeat; we soon got used to his oaths, and paid no attention to them. One day I observed to him, "I think you ought to allow us a little money to spend for ourselves." "G—d d—n your soul, you've no right to think; there are men paid to think for you," was the characteristic reply.*

Miller complained of Macdonell's rude nature and applauded his habit of defending the prisoners:

> *He was bitter, cunning and sarcastic, when he chose to be so, and I am sorry to say it, would swear most vehemently when in a rage...Some Tories who gained admittance under his wing, attempted to abuse and insult our misfortunes, but he told them plainly in our presence, "Place them on an equal footing with yourself and you will have no disposition to impose upon them a second time. They are all brave men and know how to behave themselves, and no man shall take advantage of their defenselessness to insult their feelings."*

Wright wrote of a visit by his father at Fort Henry in December 1838:

> *The sheriff refused my father the privilege of praying with any of the prisoners, and that, without regard to his age or occupation as a*

clergyman, in a most insulting manner; he however permitted him to leave me a New Testament.

In a parting letter to a friend, von Schoultz wrote:

I beg you to have printed in several of the American papers, our acknowledgement of the kindness we have experienced from the sheriff and the 83d Regiment. It is a consolation to have to deal with a brave and noble minded enemy.

Macdonell also interceded for the prisoners with a corrupt fort supplier. John Counter, thirty-nine, a local businessman and food contractor, provided meals for Fort Henry's soldiers and inmates. Poor food quality was a common complaint among prisoners, though their menu—tough beef, pea soup and coarse bread—mirrored the fare provided the enlisted men. In one case where the prisoners' food fell below the expected quality, a noisy billingsgate ensued when Sheriff Macdonell confronted Counter, as Heustis related:

Our bread, baked in [John Counter's] oven was a perfect compound of unclean ingredients. We made a complaint to Sheriff McDonald [sic] about it, and exhibited to him specimens of the dirty stuff. The Sheriff sent for Counter, and, in our presence, gave him a caustic reprimand, in which certain profane expressions were freely introduced, without much regard to the religious professions of the contractor [a devout Methodist]. In conclusion, the Sheriff ordered him to furnish better bread in future.

The sheriff allowed the captives an hour of exercise in the fort's inner parade grounds per day; otherwise, they made their own amusement.

One morning while they waited for breakfast, Henry Shew, twenty-eight, whom Heustis described as a very small man full of life and motion, bet that he could eat five men's breakfasts in no more than fifteen minutes. "Here was a chance for fun, if nothing else," wrote Heustis.

One man bet his coat, while others staked shirts, handkerchiefs and socks. Shew accepted the bets. Four men added their breakfasts and Shew's to a large pot and surreptitiously added a sixth helping:

Shew then commenced operations, while the rest of us stood by, to watch the progress of the work. At first we had hopes of winning; but these hopes were soon dissipated. Before the expiration of the time, the pan was scraped clean, and Shew declared he could have eaten more with ease.

On December 25, John Counter added a bread pudding with molasses to the Hunter prisoners' fare. Daniel Heustis had nothing pleasant to say on the topic of food, the pudding or Counter:

> *It was very dry and hard; dainty people might have refused to eat it; but such a refusal on our part would have been unreasonable, for the allowance was very small to each man, not enough, hard as it was, to baffle the digestive organs! That the philosophy of Epicurus formed no part of Mr. Counter's system of prison discipline, we had previously ascertained, to our entire satisfaction.*
>
> *But we were not prepared fully to appreciate the disinterested benevolence of the contractor, in sending us such a Christmas present, until a few days afterwards, when he presented to the Sheriff a bill for that same pudding, by which it appeared that he had charged us the nice little sum of forty dollars for the luxury!*

HANGINGS CONTINUE

Any holiday spirit abruptly ended when four American captives were hanged in the Kingston jail on January 4, 1839: Christopher Buckley; Sylvester Lawton; Russell Phelps, thirty-eight, a tailor; and Duncan Anderson, forty-eight, a laborer. Phelps and Anderson, both from Lyme, Jefferson County, were Hickory Island veterans. The British heard rumors that Phelps may have participated in the *Peel* raid.

In his memoirs, Daniel Heustis described Anderson's hanging:

> *Poor Anderson was sick, and could not have lived many weeks, if they had taken the best care of him! He was so weak that his murderers were obliged to support him on the scaffold! Comment on such atrocious barbarity is needless. In the evening, after this inhuman execution, Colonel* [Henry] *Dundas and his officers had a gay and mirthful pleasure party! O, shame! Where is thy blush?*

The day Anderson and the others died coincided with the last trial of the 161 Hunters captured after the windmill battle. Of those, Draper managed to court-martial 140 in five weeks, acquitting 4, sending 2 to prison and sentencing 134 to death. The colonial government released 16 men without trial, including

In February 1839, the Upper Canada executive council recommended to Sir George Arthur that he offer to set one hundred American prisoners free in exchange for Bill Johnston, John Birge, Lucius Bierce and William Lyon Mackenzie. And Judge Jonas Jones wrote to an American judge in Ogdensburg offering to trade one hundred Americans captured at raids near Windsor and Prescott for Mackenzie alone. To their credit, the governments of New York and the United States did not accept the offers.

wounded men and informers, among them Levi Chipman. Three wounded captives died.

By that point, 10 captured Hunters had already made the one-way trip to the gallows. In the cold, stone casements of Fort Henry, 124 others awaited their fates. Unbeknownst to them, the hangings were almost over.

LYMAN LEACH HANGED

Weeks passed following the executions of four Hunters on January 4, 1839, without additional hangings. The Fort Henry prisoners, who had seen comrades taken away to die every week or two, began to believe that the hangings had ceased.

The colonial boss, Lieutenant Governor Sir George Arthur, never intended to hang every Hunter, despite the death sentence most convicted men faced. The Upper Canada public was tiring of the brutal executions. The time approached to show mercy.

Arthur had a list of Hunters, mostly officers, whom he believed had to die as a deterrent against future raids. With ten on the list already dead, one high-priority name remained: Lyman Leach (aka Lyman Lewis). Arthur had information that Leach helped burn the *Sir Robert Peel* with Bill Johnston.

Leach may have plotted with Johnston, but he never set foot on the *Peel*. In its February 12, 1839, edition, the *Upper Canada Herald* incorrectly stated that "Lewis" was second in command at the ship's burning. True or not, people believed it. Upper Canada authorities desperately wanted to punish any associate of Bill Johnston.

Lyman grew up in the village of Cicero Center on Oneida Lake, New York. His father was an early settler there and ran a tavern in a log building. In 1813, Lyman, fifteen, enlisted to fight for America in the War of 1812.

In 1838, Lyman, forty, lived in the village of Liverpool on Onondaga Lake, where he ran a brickworks. An early Patriot recruit, he joined the brief Hickory Island occupation in February and signed up as a Hunter that summer.

Lyman often voiced his anti-British sentiments, and according to stories in the *Liverpool Telegraph*, he regularly antagonized an English immigrant named Dr. Petit:

> *The doctor was a firm believer in John Bull, and during the* [Patriot War] *espoused with ardor the cause of the British. He and Leach were often brought face to face in wordy combat and many battles of this kind were fought between them during the period of the struggle along the Canadian border. During the heated controversies, neither could find the words corresponding to their hot tempers and their feelings towards one another. The village Post Office was usually the scene of these encounters, which often ended in the doctor's prediction that if Leach ever ventured across the border he would be caught and hanged, and "damn you, Leach," he would declare, "I hope they will string you up without judge or jury."*

The doctor's prediction played out on February 11, 1839. Lyman Leach died in the Kingston jail, the eleventh and last captured windmill raider to face the gallows.

In his memoirs, Daniel Heustis wrote a paragraph summing up Lyman's strengths and failings that must serve as his epitaph as none other exists:

> *He was one of the most daring and fearless men I ever saw. He was so perfectly reckless of danger that nothing could intimidate him. Not having finished his breakfast when the officer came to escort him to the gallows, he insisted on being allowed to enjoy his last meal, and kept the officer waiting till he had coolly and deliberately concluded his repast. This heedless indifference in regard to his fate was characteristic of the man. Aside from his bravery, there were not so many attractive points in his character as were exhibited by the other martyrs.*

BILL JOHNSTON FETED IN PRISON

Following Bill Johnston's arrest at the hands of Captain William Vaughan in December 1838, he awaited trial in an Albany, New York jail cell. His faithful daughter, Kate, nineteen, moved into his cell to provide company, carry messages (she freely came and went) and attend to his needs.

Thanks to newspaper accounts of Kate's heroic efforts to avoid the navy patrols as she took supplies to her fugitive father the previous summer, Kate was as famous as Bill. Together, they entertained a steady flow of journalists, dignitaries and well-wishers. Kate reportedly turned down marriage proposals from well-to-do admirers. One newspaper account from January 26, 1839, reads in part:

> *He holds a sort of involuntary levee in his prison every day. People flock to see him, especially strangers. He is certainly a very respectable person in appearance; but there is a restlessness in his manner with a tremulousness in his eyes and an indisposition to look you honestly in the face, which gives a very unfavorable impression.*
>
> *His daughter, the adventurous girl of the Thousand Islands, is here also—the lioness of the hour. She was in the Senate Chamber the other day, the object of course of much curiosity. I am also informed she attended a ball the other evening and was well received.*

Bill's cushy treatment is an early example of celebrity incarceration. His jailers provided privileges usually reserved for the rich and famous. Visitors came and went. In his scrapbook, Bill recorded names of eighty-four people who donated money to help sustain him in prison.

On January 29, 1839, accompanied by a police escort, he attended a fundraising benefit held in his honor in Albany. He appeared at another benefit on March 5 in Auburn, New York, escorted only by Kate. The lax security was a reflection of reality. By then, Bill's jailers surely knew he'd return if he wanted to, and if not, no locks could hold him.

In mid-April 1839, a court granted Bill bail. He visited friends in New York City. At month's end, Bill returned to Clayton and ordered new boats to be built in Cape Vincent. With winter over, spring on the river proved too strong a lure: he declined to return for his court appearance.

ENGLAND FREES SOME PRISONERS BEFORE TRANSPORT

The Short Hills prisoners and other convicted Patriots jailed in England awaiting transport targeted English officials, jurists and newspapers with a

This drawing from the *London Sun*, 1839, shows rebel prisoners. From the left: Paul Bedford, Linus Miller, William Reynolds, Finlay Malcolm, John G. Parker, Randal Wixon, Leonard Watson, Ira Anderson, William Alves, James Brown, Robert Walker and John Grant.

fierce letter-writing campaign in the early months of 1839. They argued strenuously that their imprisonment was unconstitutional.

John G. Parker and eight others arrested in the panic that followed Mackenzie's Toronto attack succeeded in getting acquittals. William Reynolds was the only Short Hills raider set free following a request from the American ambassador. Miller explained his companion's good fortune as follows:

> *William Reynolds obtained a free pardon, on account, it was said, of his being the youngest of our party. He was actually three years older than myself, but had, fortunately for himself, and as unfortunately for me, stated his age when captured at eighteen years.*

Mercy was in limited supply that year, despite the fact that the Short Hills raiders killed no one and did little real damage. Benjamin Wait, Samuel Chandler, Garret Van Camp, George Cooley, James Waggoner, John Vernon, Norman Mallory, John McNulty and Alexander McLeod, with 230 common criminals, boarded the *Marquis of Hastings* on March 17, 1839, for Van Diemen's Land.

Linus Miller, John Grant, James Gammell and Jacob Beemer missed the first ship due to illness. They languished in Newgate Prison until

A young man named William Reynolds did labor at the penal colony, but he was one of the windmill raiders.

their keepers sent them to the antipodal regions onboard the *Canton* with 240 common criminals on September 22, 1839.

The first group dropped anchor in Hobarttown (now called Hobart) on July 23, 1839, and the second on January 12, 1840. All inmates paraded before the colony's lieutenant governor, Sir John Franklin. The famous arctic explorer turned prison warden lectured the assembled men and then committed them to two years of slave labor.

Laborers built roads, pushing carts laden with rocks instead of using horses or mules. They ate limited and foul rations and wore prison garb that easily fell apart. After two years, if alive, they received a "ticket to leave" that let them find work on the island for wages.

John McNulty and Alexander McLeod, two who marched on Toronto with Mackenzie, took sick on the voyage and died in Tasmania upon arrival. Garret Van Camp suffered a rupture while pushing a heavy cart and died three weeks later.

17

Windmill Prisoners Repatriated

March–June 1839

Following the execution of Lyman Leach, 146 windmill raiders, mostly Americans, continued to languish in Fort Henry. Officially, 123 faced the death sentence. As the cold grip of a Canadian winter thawed that spring, so did the Upper Canada government's chilly attitude.

In dispatches to the Home Office in England in February and April 1839, Lieutenant Governor Sir George Arthur said he intended to show clemency to the youngest prisoners as a way to soften American animosity to the colony's policies and encourage peace. He also noted that he needed to execute leaders to strike sufficient terror to forestall further invasions.

With most Hunter officers dispatched, and with public sentiment shying away from additional executions, Arthur and the colonial establishment commenced a period of repatriation.

This new policy coincided with an organized and concerted effort by American civic leaders in the border states, especially Jefferson County, to plead for mercy. They promised to prevent further raids. In conjunction, those civic leaders counseled everyone on the U.S. side to not antagonize the Upper Canada establishment.

Men of means and influence—including lawyer Bernard Bagley and Hiram Denio, co-owner of the often-hijacked *United States*—contacted colleagues and friends in Canada asking them to release specific people, often with positive results. Pardoned men, some barely literate, submitted eloquent letters to local papers on their return thanking the colonial government for its leniency. The effort paid off.

On April 8, a steamer arrived at Sackets Harbor, New York, with twenty-two prisoners, mostly teens and young men, pardoned by Sir George Arthur. Cheering friends and family, bands and dignitaries greeted them as returning heroes. On April 27, thirty-seven more pardoned men landed at Sackets Harbor to adoring crowds. Arthur sent home others in small groups, mostly wounded men not put on trial. In the end, eighty-six windmill raiders tasted freedom, leaving sixty in captivity.

In early May 1839, a list existed naming twenty-five additional men due for pardons. It included Daniel Heustis and William Gates. The pardons evaporated. Heustis acknowledged that the list existed and merely explained that it was torn up. Gates gave this version:

> *Free pardons for myself and 24 others were made out and sent down to the sheriff* [Allan Macdonell], *who, in the plenitude of his power, kept them in his own hands for two weeks. During this time, a British officer for some unknown purpose crossed the lines to French Creek* [Clayton], *in Jefferson County. Our American friends not relishing his presence treated him with that attention which they thought most befitting such gentlemen. Not having the right sort of perceptions to appreciate such honors, he became greatly enraged with the favors bestowed. Making his way back to Kingston, he gave an embittered account of the affair to the high sheriff, who forwarded a still more exaggerated report of it to the Lieutenant-Governor, accompanying it with the pardons which he had so unjustly withheld from us. The old sinner, Sir George Arthur, was so incensed that he committed them all to the flames.*

The British officer Gates mentions likely refers to Captain James Macfarlane. He escorted young Hunter Vaughan home to his father, Captain William Vaughan, in Sackets Harbor. Macfarlane, the *Kingston Chronicle* publisher and a militia officer who sat on the windmill raiders' court-martial, claimed a mob had threatened him in Oswego while he was returning home, and he had to flee for his life.

While the Macfarlane incident did arouse resentment in Upper Canada, historian John Northman presents another reason for quashing the twenty-five pardons. He wrote that on May 4, 1839, Upper Canada sheriff Alexander McMartin, fifty, escorted seven pardoned Americans (captured during a raid near Detroit in early 1838) to the border near St. Regis. Awaiting them was Judge H.W. Tucker. Instead of humbly thanking the sheriff, the judge complained of British tyranny and mistreatment of prisoners and published his diatribe. Stupidly, Tucker broke the fragile protocol upon which repatriation subsisted.

The Macfarlane and McMartin incidents made it politically impossible for Arthur to continue being lenient. He shut the door to further repatriation. Arthur did tell the inmates, through Sheriff Macdonell, that he had commuted all death sentences. Transport to Tasmania became their fate.

Lieutenant Governor Visits Captives

The man who signed the execution orders, and who had the power to pardon or transport, Lieutenant Governor Sir George Arthur, frequently visited Fort Henry to interview or lecture the prisoners. Memoirs of Fort Henry prisoners recall Arthur's visits.

Linus Miller described Arthur thus: "[He had a] stature rather below mediocrity, round shouldered, his head gray and somewhat bald, visage long, eyes small and piercing, and the general expression of his countenance perfectly passionless."

Stephen Wright said of Arthur:

> *His face was rather expressionless and of a dull withered color, and his form was rather undersized; but his eye gleamed from beneath its heavy brush with the ferocity of a bloodhound breaking cover. Not an indication of the milk of human kindness shone forth in any of his actions.*

William Gates, a man never prone to truckle to authority, became downright lippy with Arthur, as he recounted:

> *Governor Arthur came down in person to Fort Henry. To each one he addressed himself personally. Approaching where I stood, he asked my name. Being informed "Gates," said he, musingly; "Ah, your mother handed me a petition the other day for your liberation." I made no answer, for I felt in no pleasant mood. He then questioned me if I took an active part in the contest, and whether I fired at the Queen's troops, and whether I killed or intended to kill any of them. I replied to the effect that I did fire at them, and if I did not kill any of them, it was not because I had no intention. Being asked my reason, I answered that we only returned like for*

like—that her majesty's troops did what they could to shoot us. "That is enough for you," said he, as he turned away to another.

Daniel Heustis gives the following account of the same visit that Gates and Wright described:

Governor Arthur visited us once during our imprisonment. He was a short, stout-built man, and had a tyrannical look about him, which did not belie his character. Just before he left, he made a brief address to us; in which, among other things not so complimentary, he said, "If you had been fighting in the right cause, you would have been an honor to your country."

History shows that Arthur, in the end, showed far more mercy than tyranny in handling the prisoners captured at the windmill. He could have shipped the eighty-six pardoned men to Tasmania or hanged more prisoners.

MACKENZIE SWITCHES TACTICS

As early as mid-1838, William Lyon Mackenzie distanced himself from efforts to liberate Canada by force. He advocated a renewed political process. At first, Patriots paid little attention. Following multiple drubbings by the Upper Canadians and high-profile public executions in 1838 and early 1839, other Patriots began to take Mackenzie's proposal seriously.

On March 22, 1839, Mackenzie held a convention in Rochester to discuss Canada's independence. In the end, the fifty Patriot leaders in attendance formed yet another society, the Association of Canadian Refugees, with John Montgomery as president. As part of its founding charter, the group pledged to prevent further "hasty and ill-prepared expeditions or attacks" on Canada. It also specifically distanced itself from random burnings and murders (a possible reference to Benjamin Lett).

Mackenzie had little opportunity to participate further. On June 21, 1839, Judge Alfred Conklin convicted Mackenzie for violating the Neutrality Act and sent him to prison for eighteen months.

Tough Talk, No Action

Like a punch-drunk boxer who dreams of reentering the ring, Hunter and Patriot leaders in 1839 refused to admit their war was over.

According to Charles Lindsey in his biography of Mackenzie, Generals Henry Handy and Donald McLeod continued planning further armed incursions into Canada from the Detroit area in 1839. Each assured the other through letters that large numbers of men, including Indians, could be assembled in short order. (As late as October 1839, McLeod and western Patriot leaders talked confidently of another attack near Detroit.) It was all blather.

The generals exaggerated the estimates of available recruits. Stocks of weapons were in short supply because of insufficient funds. Sympathizers who once donated money to the Hunters now disavowed that organization. A handful of prominent men retained executive positions, and a hardcore group of fighters remained on the ready, but after at least ten failed invasions of Canada from Michigan to Vermont in 1838, everyone knew Canada was unassailable by a citizen army. Despite Patriot claims, no evidence shows that Native Americans were ready to risk their lives in that war.

The Patriots could still draw several thousand men to a public meeting, as they did in Watertown on February 23, 1839. The resolutions issued from the meeting did not call for war. They had more to do with publicly condemning the poor condition of Americans imprisoned in Kingston and with reaffirming American democratic ideals.

Conversely, Canada's aboriginal warriors did support Britain, as they had during the War of 1812. Among the militia units that rallied to defend Upper Canada were bands of Iroquois from the Grand River, Ojibwa from the Lake Huron area and Mohawks from eastern Lake Ontario. They participated during the Navy Island blockade, the defense of Kingston during the Hickory Island raid and the search for the Short Hills raiders. Throughout the conflict, warriors patrolled Lake Ontario and tributary rivers watching for suspicious activity.

Johnston Accused of Mail Robbery

Not every member of the crew Bill Johnston chose for his *Sir Robert Peel* raid was a bona fide Patriot. He also recruited from the ranks of vagabonds and bandits who inhabited the islands in that era.

On April 24, 1839, a long and lightweight rowboat, painted bright red inside, pale red outside and decorated with black stripes—a boat similar to Johnston's watercraft—landed in a hidden cove near Gananoque, Upper Canada. It held three burly men: Robert Smith and John Farrow, two of Johnston's old crew, and another ne'er-do-well named Washington Kelly.

They asked directions at a farm. They made inquiries concerning the mail schedule. They spent hours in a tavern. The people they met would eventually make witness against them in court.

As darkness fell, they ambushed the mail rider, Maxwell Greenwood, on his way to Kingston. With a gun pointed at the rider's chest, Kelly said he was Bill Johnston and ordered the rider down. (Though the likeness was similar, Greenwood had met Johnston and saw through Kelly's lie.)

The bandits tied Greenwood to a tree and absconded with his horse and the mail bag containing £191. Greenwood wiggled free and went to the nearest farmhouse for help.

Upper Canada complained to American authorities. Investigators suspected Kelly, Smith and Farrow but had no proof. But when the three started spending money that everyone knew they could not honestly possess, that sealed their fates.

Newspapers, especially in Upper Canada, speculated that Bill Johnston was behind the robbery. While the boat looked familiar, he had not returned from New York City by that point.

Canadians tended to blame Johnston for any crime committed near the Thousand Islands. Soon, another man became the scapegoat for all wrongdoings.

18

Windmill Prisoners Mark Time as Lett Fights On

July–December 1839

With the end of repatriation, transport to the penal colony dominated every prisoner's thoughts. Captain Heustis strived to keep up his men's spirits. That included a patriotic celebration on the Fourth of July:

> *Out of several pocket handkerchiefs a flag was manufactured, as nearly resembling the Star Spangled Banner as we could conveniently make it. This emblem of freedom and national independence we hoisted in our room, taking good care that the officers did not get a peep at it.*

Even in celebration, Heustis recalled an underlying maudlin tone:

> *We procured some lemons and sugar, which enabled us to pass round a refreshing bowl of lemonade. We then let off our toasts, in which the heroes of '76 were duly remembered. Their success had saved them from the gallows and bequeathed freedom to their posterity, while our failure had procured us a dungeon, and riveted the chains which bound the hapless Canadians as vassals of the British throne. If we had been tortured with the thought that our own cowardice had been the cause of our defeat, we should indeed have been the most miserable of men. But we had faced the enemy, as did the heroes of Bunker Hill, if not with equal success in the final result, at least in the same spirit and for the attainment of the same object, and we saw no cause for self-reproach.*

With its pale white stone and absence of any internal vegetation, Fort Henry presented a desert-like visage in the hot months of summer. As Heustis put it, "The hot and sultry days of summer, came and passed, and we still remained shut up in the gloomy prison."

Part idealist, part poet, Heustis penned the following words on the value of freedom:

> *The blessing of personal freedom, like all other blessings, is never appreciated until we feel its loss. The sick man can estimate the value of health; so can the prisoner, who has passed months in a dark and dismal cell, living on the meanest food, and breathing the foulest atmosphere, appreciate the worth of freedom. To him, wealth, honor, and renown are but idle shadows! His soul pants for liberty! Give him that, and his joyous spirit will leap forth into the world in raptures of delight!*

LETT JOINS COBOURG RAID

Late on July 26, 1839, ten Hunters carrying heavy trunks boarded a small schooner, the *Guernsey*, at Oswego, New York. The ship's posted destination was Port Credit, Upper Canada. They sailed at midnight. At daybreak, the strangers emerged on deck, drew weapons from the trunks and took over the schooner.

Benjamin Lett shared leadership with Samuel Peters Hart. Formerly a publisher of material highly critical of the Family Compact, Hart's story is familiar. He fled to America after a Tory mob wrecked his printing office and dragged him through the snow. That episode made Hart a dangerous and vengeful man.

On the morning of July 28, the *Guernsey* anchored on the north side of Lake Ontario three miles from the peaceful town of Cobourg. Hart, Lett and four others—Miles Luke, William Baker, William Watkins and Henry Wilson—disembarked. (The other four Hunters sailed on to the next port.) They journeyed to a farm run by a fellow Hunter and his son near Cobourg. There, Henry Moon, a Hunter living in Cobourg, joined them.

Lett and his gang discussed a list of victims they intended to rob, murder or abduct, including Sheppard McCormick, a participant in the *Caroline* assault. When delayed for a day waiting for repairs to a wagon, Moon reconsidered. Though he supported Hunter and Patriot goals, he couldn't be an accomplice to cold-blooded murder. He slipped away and informed Cobourg authorities.

Moon told everything he knew, which went far beyond the raid by Lett and Hart. He said an army of men in Hunter cells across Upper Canada, armed with rifles from America, would soon rise up, commandeer all Canadian steamboats on Lake Ontario and attack Upper Canada from within and without. The mastermind, according to Moon, was Bill Johnston.

Moon's description had elements of a plan Johnston and Donald McLeod might dream up. The scale was grand and the tactics clever. At that time, Johnston lurked in the Thousand Islands, acquiring boats and recruiting crews. No other evidence surfaced; Moon may have invented the story.

In Cobourg, a militia captain hastily assembled a band of armed men and rode to the farmhouse where Hart's gang reposed. Bursting in, they captured everyone but Lett and Luke, who escaped out a window and vanished in the night.

On September 13, 1839, Judge Jonas Jones convicted the Cobourg conspirators. He handed down jail terms between six months and seven years (for Hart). Moon, the prosecution's star witness, disappeared with his family. Moon had broken his Hunter oath and knew the likely consequences.

Also on September 13, someone crossed the Niagara River from New York State and burned a church in Chippewa near the home of John Ussher, brother of murdered Edgeworth Ussher. Days later, arson claimed a barn owned by a prominent loyalist. While no proof existed, locals blamed Lett. He never denied it.

JOHNSTON HUNTED AND ARRESTED, ESCAPES

As they had in the summer of 1838, the Canadian and U.S. military launched a joint patrol of the Thousand Islands in pursuit of Bill Johnston in 1839. The Americans wanted him for skipping bail—a minor consequence if captured. The Upper Canada authorities wanted him for piracy, treason and other capital crimes—all hanging offenses.

Captain Williams Sandom believed gangs of Hunters and various brigands that inhabited the islands had rallied around Johnston. Sandom had good cause. Several times, unknown men in small boats or on secluded

American islands had fired rifles at British seaman and ships. At least one cache of arms was discovered in an isolated bay on Lake Ontario.

A U.S. force, which included military observers from Upper Canada, raided Grindstone Island on July 11, 1839, to arrest Johnston. Bill escaped capture because his observant daughter Kate warned him the soldiers were coming. The raid did net a reasonable consolation prize: the mail robbers Kelly, Smith and Farrow.

A court tried, convicted and imprisoned the three mail robbers. On August 9, 1839, Kelly, Smith and Farrow escaped from jail and returned to their Thousand Islands sanctuary. They were never recaptured.

In August, Johnston visited New York City. A sharp-eyed deputy sheriff recognized and arrested him on August 19. Three days later, Bill and the deputy attended a bail hearing in Adams, New York, south of Watertown. The judge suggested bail of $10,000. Bill haggled him down to $5,000. The judge, deputy and Bill traveled to Watertown so Bill could contact his bail bondsman.

Bill's relaxed and cooperative manner through the whole arrest caused the deputy to drop his guard. In a moment of slack security, Johnston slipped away and headed for the islands.

In September 1839, the remnant Patriot leadership renewed Bill Johnston's commission. Signed by General Handy and witnessed by John Montgomery, the proclamation confirmed Johnston as admiral of the entire navy (still no ships). Bill declined.

Early in October 1839, at John Johnston's insistence, Bill returned to the Albany jail voluntarily, with Kate at his side. With cold weather coming, a cell promised far more comfort to the aging troublemaker than a fugitive winter in the Thousand Islands.

Hunters Sail for Tasmania

On September 23, 1839, blacksmiths arrived at Fort Henry after breakfast. They chained the remaining Hunter prisoners in twos at their wrists and ankles. Thirty pairs of men, mostly Americans, marched from the fort between lines of soldiers to a canalboat waiting in Navy Bay. As soon as guards secured them in the hold, they set out. A small steamer towed them up the Rideau Canal from Kingston to Ottawa and then down the Ottawa River to Montreal.

This engraving of an 1842 print by William Henry Bartlett shows Kingston from Fort Henry, with Navy Bay (foreground), the causeway and the colonial city.

The trip through the Rideau Canal and Ottawa River is far longer than the direct route down the St. Lawrence River, the route by which all previous transportees made their way to Montreal. Why choose the longer way this time? There is no official explanation. But Bill Johnston ruled the Thousand Islands, and Captain Williams Sandom believed Johnston had squads of pirates under his command. Sandom and Lieutenant Colonel Richard Bonnycastle probably expected an attack on any ship carrying Hunter prisoners.

In Montreal, the captives transferred ships and set out immediately for Quebec City, arriving the next day. In the harbor, a seven-hundred-ton sailing ship, the *Buffalo*, rode at anchor.

As guards brought each pair of shackled men onboard, Sheriff Allan Macdonell personally unlocked the wrist padlocks and wished them well. In his memoirs, Daniel Heustis regularly recorded the sheriff's humanity. Of their final parting, Heustis wrote:

I saw Sheriff McDonald [sic] standing at the gangway, and having my watch with me I inquired of him whether I should be permitted to retain it,

and if not, I wished him to send it to my friends. He gazed upon me for a
moment with a look of the deepest commiseration, and in faltering accents
told me to keep it, at the same time bursting into tears!

The *Buffalo* set sail on September 28, 1839, with the sixty windmill raiders, eighteen Patriots taken in raids near Detroit, fifty-eight Patriotes from the rebellion in Lower Canada and five common criminals.

Kept in cramped quarters through stifling tropical heat and fed rations that made the Fort Henry victuals resemble gourmet cuisine, the men arrived sick but alive in Van Diemen's Land on February 11, 1840. Among the windmill raiders, only Asa Priest, forty-five, from Auburn, New York, died on the voyage.

In Hobarttown, the penal guards unloaded the Americans and presented them to Sir John Franklin. (The *Buffalo* sailed on to Sydney, Australia, where the French Canadians disembarked on February 26.)

William Gates wrote that Franklin lectured them astride a horse for two hours, speaking in meandering, unfinished sentences while staring at the sky. The gist of his message: they were very bad men who had committed a crime worse than murder.

Guards escorted Heustis, Gates, Wright and the fifty-six other Americans to the work camps. Over the next two years, they labored in slave conditions building roads, wearing tattered clothing and eating vile and exiguous rations.

Daniel Heustis, a casement captain at Fort Henry, always held the respect and trust of his comrades. They chose him as the cell leader during the long voyage to Tasmania and as group leader at the penal colony.

Heustis's natural equanimity saved the lives and sanity of many men as he negotiated for better housing conditions, separation from the common criminals and a ban on flogging the American prisoners.

Still, men succumbed. Lysander Curtis, thirty-five, from Ogdensburg, died within weeks from overwork. Others from New York's northern counties followed him to their graves: Andrew Leeper, forty-four (Lyme); Foster Martin, thirty-five (Antwerp); Alson Owen, twenty-seven (Polermo); and Thomas Stockton, forty (Rutland).

On February 16, 1842, the penal administrators gave them tickets of leave, and the slavery period ended. They could seek paid work, and they found jobs on farms and ranches. A few escaped on American whaling ships that plied the waters. Others, including Aaron Dresser and Stephen Wright, received a pardon and money for a trip home for helping to catch bushrangers (escaped convicts who became bandits).

Between 1845 and 1848, the American prisoners received pardons. Abandoned by the U.S. government, they had to find their own way home with little money. Most worked on ships to pay for passage. At least four stayed in Tasmania or Australia. Eighteen are unaccounted for. Miraculously, the majority returned.

Eight Patriots and Hunters sent to Tasmania wrote memoirs on returning home, while others gave interviews to newspapers. None were ashamed of their actions, and all wanted the sacrifice of their comrades remembered.

19

Two Men Keep the Patriot War Alive

1840–1841

B y the end of 1839, the Hunter and Patriot movements had atrophied into a pathetic club of old men who schemed and dreamed of impossible glories. But two men kept the war in the news and Upper Canada on edge.

One was Bill Johnston. His revolving-door relationship with prison kept up the public's romantic interest in his life and the British military's hope for his capture.

The other was Benjamin Lett. He almost singlehandedly prolonged the Patriot War for another two years through a series of guerrilla raids on specific Canadian targets.

BROCK'S MONUMENT DESTROYED

Late in the day on April 16, 1840, Lett and one or two accomplices crossed into Upper Canada by boat, landing at Queenston near Niagara. His target was the stately stone spire built in 1824 to commemorate Sir Isaac Brock. Brock died while commanding the force that repelled a superior American army at the Battle of Queenston Heights in the first year of the War of 1812.

Lett's gang placed kegs of gunpowder inside the tower and, early the next morning, ignited the fuse and fled. The monument splintered from the blast. Though investigators had no evidence to tie Lett to the crime, he

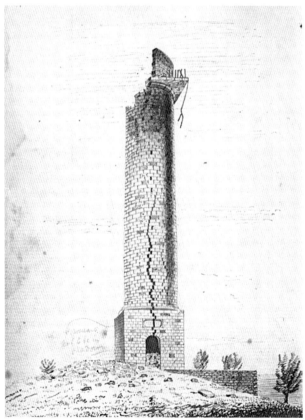

Above: This engraving of an 1840 print by William Henry Bartlett shows General Brock's monument at Queenston Heights before Benjamin Lett blew it up.

Left: Sketch of General Brock's monument at Queenston Heights after Benjamin Lett blew it up.

got the blame. Neither Benjamin nor his brother Thomas, who latter chronicled Benjamin's life, denied it. The attack fit Lett's politics and modus operandi. (The government rebuilt the monument in the 1850s.)

Sir George Arthur wrote that he had no doubt the perpetrator was Lett, whom he called the "Rob Roy of Upper Canada" after the infamous Scots bandit.

Patriot general Donald McLeod became furious upon hearing news of the monument's ruin. As a sergeant, he had served under Brock at the fateful battle and harbored deep respect for his former commander. He ordered all Patriots and Hunters to cease freelance raids. If anyone obeyed, Lett surely did not.

JOHNSTON ESCAPES ONE LAST TIME

Bill Johnston, with Kate by his side, passed the wintry months of 1839 and 1840 in the relative comfort of an Albany jail. As usual, the warm weather and wafting scents of spring stirred his vagabond soul. Bill fashioned a cell key made of zinc smuggled in by friends.

One day in late May 1840, Kate went to visit family in Rome, New York. The next evening, Bill unlocked his cell, slipped past guards and walked forty

Sketch of the Rock Island lighthouse and Bill Johnston by Benson Lossing from his book *Pictorial Field-Book of the War of 1812*, 1869.

miles before daybreak. After resting, he continued to Rome. From there, he and Kate returned to the Thousand Islands. He never saw the inside of a prison again.

Following his final escape, Johnston tried to leave his pirate and fugitive past behind. He and Kate gathered names of prominent men on a petition for a pardon. Johnston presented the petition to the outgoing president, Martin Van Buren, on March 2, 1841. He rejected Bill's plea and threatened to arrest him.

LETT BLAMED FOR EXPLOSION ON STEAMER

On June 5, 1840, the steamer *Great Britain* rested at a dock in Oswego, New York. A Canadian refugee named David Defoe carried a trunk containing explosive materials onto the steamer.

Dafoe was born in Upper Canada about 1802. A resident of Belleville, he fled Upper Canada when the rebellion started and lodged

This watercolor by Henry Francis Ainslie, 1839, shows the *Great Britain*, the largest steamer on Lake Ontario.

in Watertown, New York. He likely met Lett at a Hunter meeting or through Patriot contacts.

Defoe deposited the trunk near the ladies' cabin, lit a fuse and departed. The trunk's content—ceramic jugs of flammable liquid—exploded. A fire ensued, but people quickly extinguished the flames.

Constables arrested Defoe and Lett in Oswego that day. Their trial for arson took place on June 25. Defoe became a witness for the prosecution and blamed the whole plot on Lett. Witnesses testified that they saw Lett near the dock before the explosion. Others testified that they saw him carrying jugs similar to the fragments found at the scene.

The jury found Lett guilty, and the court sentenced him to seven years in the state prison at Auburn, New York.

While investigators proved Lett's presence near the docks, the only hard evidence of his connection to the explosion came from Defoe. Benjamin's brother Thomas later denied that his brother was involved and said Defoe had perjured himself. The bomb detonated in daylight in front of witnesses, which did not fit Lett's methodology. Of all the crimes attributed to Benjamin, the attempted destruction of the steamer—the only raid for which he was tried—may have been the one occasion he was innocent.

The train taking Lett to prison slowed going through a cedar swamp. Lett sprang from his seat, rushed through an open door and leapt into the ditch. Though heavily shackled, he disappeared into the forest.

The next day, he entered a farmhouse, revealed his identity and demanded removal of his shackles. Fearful of Lett's reputation, the farmer filed off his irons. With Lett showing no sign of leaving the following days, the farmer went for help. Lett spotted a column of men approaching, climbed out a window and fled without shoes or hat. Again, he disappeared. He had hundreds of allies and friends who would give him shelter.

LETT RECAPTURED

On September 9, 1841, a gunpowder explosion destroyed lock thirty-seven on the original Welland Canal and sank two schooners in the lock. Upper Canada authorities accused Benjamin Lett. Though blamed by many historians, Lett was innocent. American authorities had arrested him on September 6 onboard the steamer *Daniel Webster* in Buffalo as the ship readied for a westward trip. (Benjamin may have been on his way to join his siblings in Illinois.)

On September 7, constables put Benjamin Lett behind bars in Auburn, New York, where he stayed for four years.

Historian Lillian Gates stated that Lett participated in the Welland Canal conspiracy but that Dr. Edward Alexander Theller, a brigadier general with the western Patriots, actually blew up the lock.

In any case, Lett's personal war was over and with it the Patriot War. While gangs of men, calling themselves Hunters or Patriots, made short raids into Canada, they were bandits akin to John Farrow and Robert Smith, not rebels.

Lett was the last Patriot warrior standing.

Conclusion

Were the lives lost and ruined in the Patriot War all in vain? Certainly, there was no clear victory as in the Texas Revolution. For any Canadian or American who fought for freedom in 1837 and 1838, they can be forgiven for thinking it a wasted effort. But they did make a difference.

Britain's colonial masters had ignored negative reports on the dysfunctional, self-serving colonial governments in Upper and Lower Canada for years. In September 1836, for example, Dr. Charles Duncombe, then a member of the elected assembly, sailed to England with a group of reformers to take their Family Compact complaints to the seat of English colonial authority. Senior ministers showed no interest and snubbed them. Theirs was not the only vain effort at peaceful reform.

The rebellions of Upper and Lower Canada, and the fortune Britain spent fighting Patriot and Hunter invasions for a year, woke up the lounging lion. Sensing that something must be amiss, England appointed a new governor general for Canada: Lord Durham.

To his political opponents, John George Lambton, forty-six, the Earl of Durham, was known as "Radical Jack." A reformer by nature, he created a storm of protest when he submitted his report on the Canadian colonies to the Colonial Office on February 4, 1839. The report confirmed that the governments of Upper and Lower Canada consisted of corrupt, nepotistic and elitist cliques.

He made two main recommendations: replace the corrupt executive councils with a cabinet composed of elected members, and unite Upper and Lower Canada.

Scarcely had the ink dried on his report, than Lord Durham died of tuberculosis on July 28, 1840.

The British government of the day balked at abolishing the existing appointed executive councils. It took a change in England's ruling party in 1847 before responsible government came to the Canadian colonies.

Britain did move quickly on the second part. In 1840, it created a single colony called the United Province of Canada, or simply Canada, with the first election held in 1841.

One paragraph in Lord Durham's report won the hearts of Canadian rebellion refugees and their American friends by confirming what they knew to be true:

> *It certainly appeared too much as if the rebellion had been purposely invited by the Government, and the unfortunate men who took part in it deliberately drawn into a trap by those who subsequently inflicted so severe a punishment on them for their error. It seemed, too, as if the dominant party made use of the occasion afforded it by the real guilt of a few desperate and imprudent men, in order to persecute or disable the whole body of their political opponents. A great number of perfectly innocent individuals were thrown into prison, and suffered in person, property and character. The whole body of reformers was subjected to suspicion, and to harassing proceedings instituted by magistrates whose political leanings were notoriously averse to them. Severe laws were passed under color of which individuals very generally esteemed were punished without any form of trial.*

It is the nature of Canadian politics that change comes slowly through negotiation and compromise, not revolution. The Patriot War did not win freedom immediately, but it made the political masters fix a problem they had too long ignored and far sooner than would have occurred otherwise. The Patriot War forced a change in governance in favor of democratic institutions and created fertile ground for the creation of an independent Canada in 1867.

What Happened To...

After the Patriot War, the survivors went on with their lives—for decades or mere years—where Fate bestowed honors, ignominy, prosperity, penury, fame or obscurity.

SIR GEORGE ARTHUR (June 21, 1784–September 19, 1854): Arthur left Upper Canada for England in 1841 and was made a baronet as a reward. (He had already been knighted for his service in Van Diemen's Land.) In 1842, the government posted him to India as governor of Bombay. Later, England promoted him to major general and made him a member of the Privy Council.

BERNARD BAGLEY (November 5, 1791–June 26, 1878): Following the Patriot War, Bagley dabbled in politics, serving as Pamelia supervisor and a state assembly member. Bagley, William Estes and twenty others were founding trustees of the Jefferson County Savings Bank incorporated on April 5, 1859. His involvement with raiders and pirates must have embarrassed his family. Bagley's detailed and effusive obituary in the *Watertown Daily Times* on June 27, 1878, made no reference to his extensive support for the Patriot movement. He is buried in the Brookside Cemetery in Watertown.

ELIZABETH BARNETT (1815–August 23, 1906): On March 14, 1838, just weeks after her heroic journey across the ice to warn of an impending Hunter invasion, Barnett married Warren Fairman of Howe Island, one of the militiamen sent to guard Gananoque. They had eleven children and grew very old together. She died at ninety-one, and he died in 1909 at ninety-three.

JACOB BEEMER: Beemer was born about 1810 in Upper Canada. In Tasmania, his pardon stalled until 1848 due to bad behavior. He remained in Tasmania, where, at thirty-eight, he married Ann Walker, eighteen (despite having a wife in Canada). They had three children. After Ann died, Beemer married a second time and sired two more children. He never came home.

JOHN WARD BIRGE (December 9, 1807–October 16, 1873): Birge disappeared after his prison escape in 1838 and kept a low profile for twenty-three years. At the start of the Civil War, Birge (then in St. Louis) jumped into the fight. Between August and November 1861, he raised an elite regiment of marksmen called the Western Sharpshooters. The regiment fought the entire war for the Union with distinction. Birge commanded it for less than a year, being discharged in March 1862.

SIR FRANCIS BOND HEAD (January 1, 1793–July 20, 1875): After leaving Canada, Bond Head never held another public position. He established himself as an odd but mildly successful writer. As a belated reward for his "service," Queen Victoria made him a member of her Privy Council in 1867.

SIR RICHARD BONNYCASTLE (September 30, 1791–November 2, 1847): A grateful Britain knighted him in 1840 and promoted him from regimental major to lieutenant colonel. He remained in Kingston, where he penned several books.

SAMUEL CHANDLER (October 8, 1791–March, 29 1866): Chandler and Benjamin Wait escaped Tasmania by rowing out to an American whaling ship on Christmas Day 1841. They survived a shipwreck in Brazil. Befriended by another American captain, they arrived at New York in July 1842. Masons paid their train fare to Niagara Falls, where they united with their families. Chandler settled at Bridgeport, Iowa, in 1843 with his wife, Hannah, and thirteen children. He lived out his life as a farmer and miller, dying of kidney failure in 1866. In 1906, historians erected a monument to him near his former Ontario home.

JOHN COUNTER (April 18, 1799–October 29, 1862): Despite being a supplier of substandard food, Counter was a successful businessman in Kingston, involved in land sales, shipbuilding and ferry services. He served terms as mayor. He fell on hard times in his latter years and died poor and nearly forgotten. A major Kingston street bears his name.

DR. CHARLES DUNCOMBE (July 28, 1792–October 1, 1867): After the Patriot cause collapsed, Dr. Duncombe stayed in the northern states, lecturing and practicing medicine. Though pardoned by Canada in 1843, he never returned. He settled in Sacramento in 1849 and served terms in the California legislature. He died of complications from sunstroke.

LIEUTENANT COLONEL HENRY DUNDAS (February 25, 1801–February 1, 1876): Dundas received a knighthood and a promotion to full colonel for his role at the Battle of the Windmill, despite the fact that he did little but show up. He became Third Viscount Melville on his father's death in 1851.

CHARLES DURAND (April 9, 1811–August 16, 1905): Arrested in Hamilton in December 1837 for no more than associating with reformers, Durand spent nine months in jail, often severely ill, before being exiled to America in August 1838. With his young wife, Sarah Bostwick (they had four children), he settled in Chicago. Pardoned in 1844, he returned to Toronto and became a prominent member of the legal community. He published his memoirs in 1897.

WILLIAM ESTES (September 1, 1803–July 13, 1881): Following the Patriot War, Estes served as supervisor of Cape Vincent in 1857 and as a justice of the peace in 1877. He was a founding trustee of the Jefferson County Savings Bank in April 1859. Throughout his life, he retained the title "General." His grave in the old Market Street cemetery in Cape Vincent bears the label "Gen. William Estes."

SILAS FLETCHER (September 1, 1780–May 12, 1847): After the Patriot War, Fletcher settled south of Dunkirk, New York, where he remained for life. He is buried in the Laona Cemetery in Chautauqua County.

MARSHALL W. FORWARD (1817–August 15, 1884): Following his release from jail as a *Peel* raider in 1838, Forward kept a low profile. By 1843, he was established in Oswego, New York, as a lumber merchant, a profession he kept for life. Forward married Maria Louisa Bickford in 1841. They had at least one child.

LIEUTENANT WILLIAM NEWTON FOWELL (June 5, 1803–June 17, 1868): Fowell joined the Patriot War in August 1838 under Captain Williams Sandom. For his brilliant defense of Canada on the *Experiment*, he was promoted to commander. He succeeded Sandom in the summer of 1843 as naval commander. He returned to England in 1848 and retired as a captain in 1852. The naval seniority system ultimately made him a rear admiral by 1867.

COLONEL RICHARD DUNCAN FRASER (1784–April 1, 1857): As the customs collector in Brockville, Fraser was at the center of a diplomatic mishap in May 1839 that nearly restarted the shooting war. He seized an American schooner for failing to declare an artillery piece as part of its cargo. He relented only after staring down the cannon of an American warship that came to the schooner captain's aid. Later, an audit of his books at the customhouse showed he had not handed over all customs duties collected. He blamed Bill Johnston for stealing the money. No one believed him, and he lost the position in January 1843. He retreated to his farm with his wife, Mary (McDonell).

SAMUEL CHALLOTT FREY (February 1799–February 24, 1877): After his release from jail in 1838, Frey moved his wife, Susan (Calhoun), and three children to Canton, Ohio, and set up a jewelry business. His eldest son, George, became a prominent businessman, newspaper publisher, an early investor in the telegraph and, eventually, president of the board of county commissioners. Samuel and Susan moved to Springfield, Ohio, and later to Decatur, Alabama, where they lived out their lives.

WILLIAM GATES (1814–1865?): Pardoned in September 1845, Gates went to Australia. He labored on a farm for two years to earn his fare home. Arriving in America on May 31, 1848, he traveled overland to the family home in Cape Vincent. His parents had moved, his eldest brother had died and his siblings had scattered. He located his parents in the Canadian village of Aylmer, south of London. He paid them a visit, ironically traveling part way on the steamer *Experiment*. He convinced his parents to return to America. They settled in Wilson, New York. In 1850, Gates published his memoirs with details of the battle and his imprisonment in Tasmania.

APPENDIX

DAVID GIBSON (March 9, 1804–January 25, 1864): After, the rebellion, Gibson established a surveying business in Lockport, New York, and brought his wife and two sons there. He worked on the Erie Canal construction as an engineer. Though pardoned by Britain in 1843, he stayed in the United States until 1848. He returned to Canada as a surveyor and also became a prosperous farmer and mill owner. Dr. John Rolph appointed him inspector of Crown land agencies and superintendent of colonial roads. In his lifetime, he surveyed major sections of eight counties in central Ontario and laid out principal colonial roads.

DANIEL DUNBAR HEUSTIS (April 8, 1806–1853): Pardoned late in 1844, Heustis and twenty-six other ex-Hunters departed from Tasmania on a whaling ship on January 29, 1845. After a journey that took him to the Antarctic waters, California and South America, he arrived in Boston on June 25, 1846. Back in Watertown, he learned that his first wife, Mary Ann Wilkinson, had divorced him to remarry. In Westmoreland, New Hampshire, he met Mary Starkey, eighteen. They wed on November 19, 1847. The couple, with Daniel's mother, Abigail, moved to Wayne County, Michigan, where Daniel worked as a police officer. They had a daughter. According to family records, he died in 1853 during one of the periodic cholera outbreaks, an ironic ending for a man who had survived the filth and pestilence of prison ships and slavery.

CATHERINE "KATE" JOHNSTON (September 11, 1819–March 14, 1878): For her era, Kate married late in life, perhaps because she didn't want to abandon her tomboy life on the river. At twenty-nine, she wed Charles Hawes (1819–1872) on February 21, 1848. They had a least five children. Kate is buried in the family plot.

WILLIAM "BILL" JOHNSTON (February 1, 1782–February 17, 1870): Despite his bandit reputation, Johnston's War of 1812 contributions still carried weight. The U.S. government awarded him the plum patronage job of Rock Island lighthouse keeper. He held that position from April 12, 1853, to April 8, 1861. After that, he ran a tavern on Whiskey Island. He spent the last years of his life living in the Walton House, a hotel owned by his son, Samuel Decatur. Bill is buried in the family plot just south of Clayton.

PRESTON KING (October 14, 1806–November 12, 1865): Born in Ogdensburg, King studied law, started a newspaper and was elected to the state government all as a young man. After the Patriot War, he continued in politics, serving in both the Congress and the Senate. He committed suicide by leaping from a ferryboat in New York Harbor. He is buried in the City Cemetery, Ogdensburg.

BENJAMIN LETT (November 14, 1813–December 9, 1858): While Benjamin terrorized Canada, his mother and siblings left Canada for Texas early in 1838, likely to escape persecution for Benjamin's deeds. In 1839, Lett's siblings (their mother having died) moved to Louisiana and then to LaSalle County, Illinois, in 1840. His devoted brother, Thomas (June 17, 1809–July 8, 1885), worked hard for his brother's early release as Benjamin fell ill in the harsh prison conditions. New York governor Silas Wright pardoned Lett on March 10, 1845. Benjamin moved to the family farm and left his terrorist life behind. He died under mysterious circumstances in Milwaukee. Thomas claimed agents of the Canadian government lured him away and poisoned him with strychnine. William Lyon Mackenzie sent a letter of condolence, adding that Benjamin "was warm-hearted and brave as Man can be."

JOHN ALEXANDER MACDONALD (January 11, 1815–June 6, 1891): Macdonald began a career in politics in 1843. His first wife (they married on September 1, 1843), Isabella Clark, died in 1857. They had two sons. He married Susan Agnes Bernard on February 16, 1867. They had one daughter. Thirty years after the start of the Patriot War, Macdonald became the first prime minister of an independent Canada and led it through its first formative decades. He was knighted on Canada's first birthday, July 1, 1867.

WILLIAM LYON MACKENZIE (March 12, 1795–August 28, 1861): Relegated to the sidelines (or preferring to be there) during the rebellion, Mackenzie continued publishing his polemics when his funds allowed. He spent eleven months in prison (1839–1840) for breaking the U.S. Neutrality Act. After his pardon in February 1849, he returned to Toronto and spent another seven years, from 1851 to 1858, as a member of the colonial legislature. Though the Family Compact was gone and many reforms enacted, he never stopped demanding equality for all and an end to favoritism. His grandson, William Lyon Mackenzie King, served as Canada's tenth and longest-sitting prime minister. His terms in office covered parts of the Great Depression and World War II.

DONALD MCLEOD (January 1, 1779–July 22, 1879): Britain pardoned McLeod in 1846. He returned to Canada and took a federal government job. After retirement, he moved to Cleveland, Ohio, where he remained until dying in his 101st year.

LINUS WILSON MILLER (December 28, 1817–April 11, 1880): Miller left Tasmania in September 1845 and landed in Delaware on January 25, 1846. He journeyed to Stockton, New York, to find his parents and siblings alive and well. Miller, still a young man, picked up the threads of his life. He wrote his memoirs and became a farmer and dairyman. In January 1850, he married Anne Jeanette Curtis. They had two sons and three daughters.

JOHN MONTGOMERY (February 29, 1788–October 31, 1879): Britain pardoned Montgomery in 1843. He returned to Toronto and built a large tavern on the site of the old one on Yonge Street. In 1871, he moved to Markham Township (northeast of Toronto), where he was postmaster. In 1873, the Ontario government awarded him $3,000 for the loss of his tavern in 1837. At his trial in 1838, when asked if he had anything to say, Montgomery accused witnesses of perjury. He cursed the judge, jury and prosecutors vowing that, when they had "perished in hell's flames, John Montgomery will yet be living on Yonge Street." When Montgomery died, he had outlived the judge, prosecutors and most jurors and witnesses.

LIEUTENANT CHARLES ALLAN PARKER (September 13, 1813–September 4, 1854): Parker departed the Canadians colonies in November 1840. In England, he married Martha E. Simpson on September 8, 1846. They had four children. He became a captain in 1847. During the Crimean War, Parker, forty, sailed in a fleet that attacked Petropavlovsk in far eastern Russia. He died leading his men in a fruitless assault on a hill and is buried there. One of the editors of his memoirs, Rosalyn Parker Art, is his great-great-granddaughter.

JOHN GOLDSWORTHY PARKER (May 14, 1794–June 24, 1875): After being shipped out of Canada in November 1838, Parker spent six months waiting in England's dreary Newgate Prison for the trip to Tasmania. Parker, Leonard Watson and seven other prisoners arrested for the original uprisings in December 1837 appealed their convictions. In July 1839, English courts released them ruling that their imprisonment was illegal. John rejoined his family in America and set up business as a grocer in Rochester, New York.

Oliver Beale Pierce (December 25, 1808–June 5, 1865): Born in Massachusetts, he lived most of his life in Rome, New York. As a grammar specialist, he lectured widely and wrote a book titled *Pierce's Grammar*. For a time he was editor of the *Rome Excelsior* and the *Rome Vigilant*. He dabbled in inventions and has a patent registered for a fire safety staircase. At least one report stated that his home in Rome was a stop on the Underground Railroad. He is buried in the Rome cemetery.

Dr. John Rolph (March 4, 1793–October 19, 1870): Rolph stepped away from the Patriot War early in 1838 and moved to Rochester, New York, where his wife, Grace (they had four children), joined him. Pardoned in 1843, he returned to Toronto to practice and teach medicine. Rolph won more terms as a member of the assembly and had a stint as commissioner of Crown lands and as minister of agriculture while continuing in medicine. A stroke in 1861 cut into his heavy professional schedule.

Captain Williams Sandom (1785–August 15, 1858): Despite his brilliant efforts to defend Canada in 1838, Sandom received no recognition or promotion. His famous choleric temper may have been the cause. Embittered that the spoils of war went to lesser lights, he returned to England in 1843. Through the navy's seniority system, he became a rear admiral in 1854.

Hugh Scanlan: (1810–?) Little is known of Scanlan. John Haddock, in his 1895 history of Jefferson County, described Scanlan (aka Scanlon) as "an Irish-Canadian, a bright and shrewd fellow." According to Sir Richard Bonnycastle, Scanlan was "an absconding debtor from Kingston." After skipping bail in 1838, he eventually settled in New York City. Beginning in 1854, his name appears on New York City documents as a licensed dealer in second-hand goods (chiefly furniture) at 215 Canal Street. He married and had two daughters and a son. He was still alive at the time of the 1870 federal census.

Henry Shew (October 14, 1809–?): When Shew returned from Tasmania to Wilna, Jefferson County (circa 1852), he discovered that his wife, Margaret Stata, had assumed him dead and remarried. Henry visited relatives and got to know his son, Wilson. Without telling relatives where he was going, Henry disappeared. His descendents say he did not want to break up his former wife's new home.

NELSON TRUAX (March 23, 1818–January 25, 1915): Sir George Arthur pardoned Truax in May 1838. He returned to Watertown and resumed his trade as harness maker. On February 23, 1847, he married Sarah Whitney. They had five children. Truax enlisted in the Fourth New York Infantry in 1861 and served for the duration of the Civil War. When he died at ninety-six, he was the last Hunter veteran of the windmill battle. He rests in the North Watertown Cemetery.

JAMES VAN CLEVE (1808–April 21, 1888): Van Cleve was born in Lawrenceville, New Jersey, and moved with his family to Batavia, New York, in 1809. He was a natural naval man. He attained his captaincy in 1830 while still in his early twenties. Following the Battle of the Windmill, the owners of the *United States* blamed Van Cleve for aiding the rebels and fired him. He got other commands and continued as a captain until about 1850. He became general manager of the Ontario and St. Lawrence Steamboat Company. He married Harriet Barton, and they had at least one child. Van Cleve, who made sketches most of his adult life, went on to be a respected local artist specializing in paintings of ships and harbors. He died in his eightieth year in Sandwich, Ontario.

RENSSELAER VAN RENSSELAER (March 1802–January 1, 1850): Van Rensselaer spent six months in jail for his role in early raids on Canada. After his release, he married Euphemia "Mary" Foreman in November 1840. They had one child. He committed suicide by inhaling charcoal gas (carbon monoxide poisoning) on January 1, 1850.

BENJAMIN WAIT (September 7, 1813–November 9, 1895): Wait and Samuel Chandler escaped from Tasmania in 1841 and landed in New York in 1842. (See Samuel Chandler for details of the trip.) Wait published his memoirs in 1843 as a series of contrived letters between Wait and his wife, Maria. Maria, who never stopped fighting for his freedom, died in May 1843 after giving birth to twins. Wait remarried in 1845 and moved to Grand Rapids, Michigan. He became a lumberman and founded the *Northwestern Lumberman* magazine in 1873. He later lost his fortune and lived on charity for his final years.

Bibliography

This bibliography comes in three sections. Section one lists firsthand accounts—the journals, notes, letters and memoirs—of people who participated in the Patriot War. The second part lists works by observers who lived in the era and recorded events or interviewed participants. The third part consists of sources by later historians.

FIRSTHAND ACCOUNTS

Andrews, Robert J., and Rosalyn Parker Art, eds. *A Troublesome Berth: The Journal of First Lieutenant Charles Parker, Royal Marines: The Canada Years, 1838–1840.* Kingston, Ontario: Kingston Historical Society, 2009. [Parker participated in the Battle of the Windmill.]

Gates, William. *Recollections of Life in Van Diemen's Land.* Lockport, NY: George Mackaness, 1850. [Gates participated in the Battle of the Windmill.]

Miller, Linus W. *Notes of an Exile to Van Diemen's Land.* Fredonia, NY: W. McKinstry & Co., 1846. [Miller participated in the Short Hills raid.]

A Narrative of the Adventures and Sufferings of Captain Daniel D. Heustis. Boston: Silas W. Wilder & Co., 1848. [Heustis participated in the Hickory Island raid and the Battle of the Windmill.]

Proceedings of the Militia General Court Martial, Fort Henry 1838, RG5 B41. Library and Archives Canada (microfilm). [Provides transcripts of the trials of men captured at the Battle of the Windmill.]

Reminiscences of Charles Durand. Toronto, ON: Hunter, Rose Co., 1897.

Wait, Benjamin. *Letters from Van Diemen's Land Written during Four Year Imprisonment for Political Offences Committed in Upper Canada*. Buffalo, NY: W.W. Wilgus, Buffalo, 1843. [Wait participated in the Short Hills raid.]

Wright, Stephen S. *Narrative and Recollections of Van Diemen's Land during Three Years' Captivity*. Edited by Caleb Lyon. New York: New World Press, 1844. [Wright participated in the Battle of the Windmill.]

OBSERVERS' ACCOUNTS

Bonnycastle, Sir Richard. *Canada As It Was, Is and Will Be*. Edited by Sir James Edward Alexander. London: Colburn and Co., 1852. [This posthumously published book includes many details of British activities in the Thousand Islands during the Patriot War.]

Canniff, Dr. William. *History of the Settlement of Upper Canada*. Toronto, ON: Dudley & Burns, 1869. [Canniff interviewed people who knew Bill Johnston, including his eldest brother, James.]

Hough, Franklin B. *A History of Jefferson County, New York*. Albany, NY: Joel Munsel, 1854. [Hough interviewed Bill Johnston about the *Peel* raid. Other passages confirm events of the Patriot War.]

Lindsay, Charles. *Life and Times of Wm. Lyon Mackenzie*. Toronto, ON: P.R. Randall, 1862. [Lindsey, Mackenzie's son-in-law, wrote the biography using William's notes. For the most part, the book is a wealth of Patriot War information. Lindsey incorrectly stated that Bill Johnston captained one of the Hunter schooners during the Prescott attack. Every historical account I have read from John Charles Dent in 1885 up to the end of the twentieth century repeated that mistake. Donald E. Graves fixed the historical record in 2001 in *Guns Across the River*.]

Lossing, Benson J. *Pictorial Field-Book of the War of 1812*. New York: Harper & Brothers, 1869. [Lossing interviewed Bill Johnston a year before his death.]

HISTORICAL ACCOUNTS

Dent, John Charles. *Upper Canadian Rebellion.* Toronto, ON: C. Blackett Robinson, 1885.

Dictionary of Canadian Biography Online. http://www.biographi.ca/index-e.html. [Provided valuable details on the lives of many people mentioned in this book.]

Dunley, Ruth. "In Search of A.D. Smith, A Detective's Quest," *Wisconsin Magazine of History*, volume 89, number 2, winter 2005-2006.

FitzGibbon, Mary Agnes. *Veteran of 1812, the Life of James FitzGibbon.* Toronto, ON: William Briggs, 1894.

Fuller, L.N. "Northern New York in the Patriot War." Published in serial form in the *Watertown Daily Times*, 1923.

Gates, Lillian. *After the Rebellion: The Later Years of William Lyon Mackenzie.* Quebec: Gagne Printing, 1988.

Graves, Donald E. *Guns Across the River.* Prescott, ON: Friends of Windmill Point, 2001. [Graves compiled the most thorough history of the Battle of the Windmill, including the names of most participants on both sides.]

Guillet, Edwin G. *The Lives and Times of the Patriots.* Toronto: Ontario Publishing Co., 1938, 1963.

Haddock, John. *History of Jefferson County.* Albany, NY: Weed-Parson, 1895.

———. *The Thousand Islands of the St. Lawrence River from Kingston and Cape Vincent to Morristown and Brockville.* Albany, NY, 1895.

Moses, John. *A Sketch Account of Aboriginal Peoples in the Canadian Military.* With Donald E. Graves and Warren Sinclair. Department of National Defence Canada, 2004.

New York History 65, no. 2 (April 1964). [Includes a detailed article by Laurence Goodrich on Randall Palmer with information on his Johnston portrait.]

Northman, John, pseudo. "Pirates of the Thousand Islands." Published in serial form in the *Watertown Daily Times*, 1938–39. [This series, by Toronto author W.J. Wraith, is the only published biography of Bill Johnston.]

Stage 1 Archaeological Assessment, McBurney Park, Upper Burial Ground, Kingston, Ontario. Cataraqui Archaeological Research Foundation, 2003.

In addition, numerous genealogy sites available on the Internet provided valuable details on the lives of many people described in this book.

Index

About the Author

S haun McLaughlin maintains two history blogs: one on the Patriot War and other Canadian-American border clashes and one on William Johnston, the Thousand Islands legend. A researcher, journalist and technical writer for over thirty years, with a master's degree in journalism, he lives on a hobby farm in Eastern Ontario. Now a semiretired freelance writer, he focuses on fiction and nonfiction writing projects.

Visit us at
www.historypress.net